EVALUATING THE EFFECTIVENESS OF COMMUNITY PENALTIES

**Books are to be returned on or before
the last date below.**

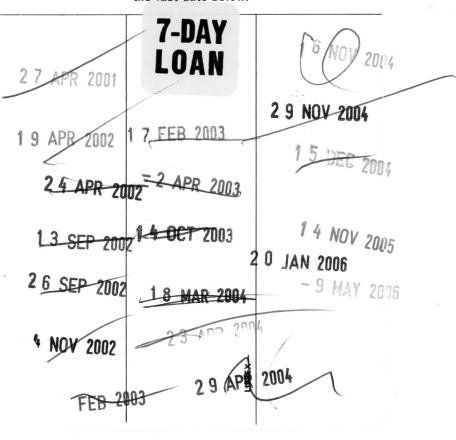

**7-DAY
LOAN**

27 APR 2001

6 NOV 2004

29 NOV 2004

19 APR 2002   17 FEB 2003

15 DEC 2004

24 APR 2002   2 APR 2003

13 SEP 2002   14 OCT 2003

14 NOV 2005

20 JAN 2006

26 SEP 2002   18 MAR 2004

- 9 MAY 2006

4 NOV 2002   23 APR 2004

FEB 2003   29 APR 2004

Evaluating the Effectiveness of Community Penalties

Edited by
GEORGE MAIR
School of Law, Social Work & Social Policy
Liverpool John Moores University

Avebury

Aldershot • Brookfield USA • Hong Kong • Singapore • Sydney

Published by
Avebury
Ashgate Publishing Limited
Gower House
Croft Road
Aldershot
Hants GU11 3HR
England

Ashgate Publishing Company
Old Post Road
Brookfield
Vermont 05036
USA

British Library Cataloguing in Publication Data

Evaluating the effectiveness of community penalties. -
    (Evaluative studies in social work)
    1.Community service (Punishment) - Great Britain -
    Evaluation 2.Probation - Government policy - Great Britain
    3.Community-based corrections - Great Britain - Evaluation
    I.Mair, George
    364.6'8'0941

Library of Congress Catalog Card Number: 96-079949

ISBN 1 85972 025 0

Printed and bound by Athenaeum Press, Ltd.,
Gateshead, Tyne & Wear.

Contents

Tables and Figures

Preface

Evaluative Studies in Social Work brings together research which has explored the impact of social work services in a variety of contexts and from several perspectives. The vision of social work in this series is a broad one. It encompasses services in residential, fieldwork and community settings undertaken by workers with backgrounds in health, welfare and criminal justice. The volumes will therefore include studies of social work with families and children, with elderly people, people with mental and other health problems and with offenders.

This approach to social work is consistent with contemporary legislation in many countries, including Britain, in which social work has a key role in the assessment of need and in the delivery of personal social services, in health care and in criminal justice. It also continues a long tradition which perceives an integral relationship between social work, social research and social policy. Those who provide social work services are acquainted with the complexities of human need and with the achievements and shortcomings of major instruments of social policy. This knowledge was exploited by, amongst others, Booth, Rowntree and the Webbs in their studies of poverty. Politicians and sociologists have also recognised that, together with the people they try to help, social workers can provide a commentary on the human meaning of public policies and the social issues that grown from private troubles.

This knowledge and experience of the recipients and practitioners of social work, is not, of course, immediately accessible to the wider community. A major purpose of research is to gather, organise and interpret this information and, in the studies in this series, to evaluate the impact of social work. Here there are many legitimate interests to consider. First and foremost are direct service users and those who care for them. These are the people who should be the main beneficiaries of social work services. Also to be considered are the personnel of other services for whom liaison and collaboration with social work is essential to their own successful functioning. The needs and views of these different groups may well conflict and it is the researcher's task to identify those tensions and describe social work's response to them.

The problems which confront social work are often extremely complex. They may need to be tackled in a variety of ways; for example, through practical assistance, advocacy, counselling and supervision. Outcomes may be similarly varied and studies of the effectiveness of social work must demonstrate the different kinds of impact it can have. These may entail changes in users' circumstances, behaviour or well being. On these changes, and on the kind of help they have received, users' perspectives must be of great significance. Also of central interest to those who provide or manage services is an understanding of their form and content and the relationship between the problems identified and the statutory responsibilities of social workers and the help given. Social work researchers must therefore take care to study what is actually delivered through social work and how, as well as its outcomes, aspirations and objectives. For good and ill social work has an impact on large and increasing number of citizens. A major aim of *Evaluative Studies in Social Work* is to increase well informed understanding of social work, based on knowledge about its real rather than imagined activities and outcomes.

The identification of effectiveness, in its various forms, can also not be the end of the story. The costs of the associated services must be studied, set in the context of their effectiveness, to allow the most efficient use of resources.

These demands present major challenges to researchers who have to use, adapt and develop a wide range of research methods and designs. Ingenuity and persistence are both required if evaluative research in social work is to be pursued in contexts often regarded as beyond the scope of such enquiry. *Evaluative Studies in Social Work* intends to make widely available not only the research findings about the impact of social work but also to demonstrate and discuss possible approaches and methods in this important and developing field of enquiry.

The first volumes in this study described studies undertaken in the Social Work Research Centre established at the University of Stirling in 1986. With funds from the Economic and Social Research Council, the Scottish Office and the University itself the Centre evaluates the effectiveness of social work services using a variety of methodology approaches.

Evaluating the Effectiveness of Community Penalties is the first edited collection in this series; it is also the first volume to include accounts of research undertaken outside the Social Work Research Centre. The publication of these papers is remarkable for several reasons.

First of all they provide ample demonstration of the methodological sophistication which has been achieved through the several decades of international evaluation research which has focused on community penalties and which increasingly takes account of the perspectives of their many different interest groups. McIvor's and Raynor's chapters illustrate well the importance of this accumulated experience in establishing viable community based programmes and in avoiding premature judgements of what does and does not 'work'. The chapter by Mair, Lloyd and Hough on the complexity of the determination and interpretation of reconviction rates is another example of the standards which should be adhered to - but which often are not - by those whose research and policy making tangle with accounts of further offending.

Methodological sophistication does not necessarily mean achieving the ideals of evaluative research, particularly given the increased subtlety of the questions posed. It also includes grasping the limitations of available research methods and designs in capturing both the process and impact of community based approaches to the control of crime and to helping offenders. Particularly difficult to establish is a robust account of the processes of intervention and the real relationship between intervention and outcome. These problems are explored in the chapters on the 'Tackling Offending Initiative' by James and Bottomley; in Mair's evaluation of intensive probation; in Williams' and Creamer's study of special Scottish probation schemes and in Hine's exploration of community service orders. Clear's study of American intensive probation is a timely reminder that priority goals can exclude any intended help for offenders and of the impact of local communities on the shape of community penalties. All these studies are excellent examples of carefully designed responses to evaluation which include sober analysis of their shortcomings and of the conclusions which can and cannot be drawn from them. They demonstrate the value of responding to the imperative of evaluation with the best available means and making acknowledged deficiencies a platform for further improvement in research design. Knapp's and Netten's account of studying the costs of community penalties in the context of their effectiveness demonstrates well the gains of daring and pioneer analysis.

These research achievements deserve recognition. They show that amongst social work services the evaluation of interventions directed at offenders is generally more advanced than the evaluation of provision for other groups such as parents and children and elderly people. Such celebrations, modest though they be, must not generate complacency, as Pawson's chapter eloquently argues. Evaluative research still has a long way to travel before it can move from rather general identification of effective approaches in programmes for offenders to providing more subtle and differentiated responses to questions about which aspects of programmes are more likely to be effective for which sort of people. The last chapter in this collection therefore appropriately poses a challenge for further researchers to explore the potential of 'scientific realist evaluation' to unravel both the different components of intervention - and the varying characteristics of their recipients - and to determine why certain approaches appear to be more or less effective, and in what context.

The publication of these papers is also remarkable for their relevance to policy analysis and development. Mair's introduction and the following chapter by McIvor show the progress that has been made in practitioners' and policy makers' responses to the conclusions of researchers. They also outline the priorities for studies which continue to meet the demands of relevance and acknowledge the complexity of the real world of policy and practice. They and other authors map the terrain, albeit sometimes rough, for a rational approach to policy making and to research based practice. The fact that policy makers, for political and ideological reasons, choose to go down quite contrary paths must not deter us from continuing to amass and to disseminate - at all appropriate levels - knowledge about effective programmes for offenders whose threat to civil society now receives so much attention and whose needs so little. The research described in this volume gives grounds for optimism about further evaluative achievements. These are not a sufficient condition for rational and effective penal policy but they are an absolutely necessary one.

Juliet Cheetham

Acknowledgements

This book has had a lengthy gestation process and I am grateful to the contributors for their patience as I struggled with the pressures of work in the Home Office Research and Planning Unit and then all of the problems associated with a new job. I am also grateful to my colleagues in the School of Law, Social Work and Social Policy at John Moores University for welcoming me and helping to make the transition from civil service to academia as stress-free as possible. Pam Lavery and Gill McIvor of the Social Work Research Centre at the University of Stirling have been immensely helpful. The support of various other individuals has been invaluable in a variety of ways, but I do not propose to embarrass them by naming them here - its a case of the usual suspects and they know who I'm talking about.

George Mair
May 1996

Contributors

Keith Bottomley is Professor of Criminology at the University of Hull. He is the author of many books and articles on the criminal justice system, and is particularly well known for his research on prisons.

Todd R. Clear is Professor and Associate Dean in the School of Criminology and Criminal Justice, Florida State University. Previously he was Professor in the School of Criminal Justice at Rutgers University. He is the author of numerous books and articles on community corrections including *Controlling the Offender in the Community* and *Harm in American Penology*. In 1986 he was the recipient of the Cincinnati Award of the American Probation and Parole Association for his research on supervision technologies.

Anne Creamer is a lecturer in Social Work at the University of Dundee. Her research interests focus on the monitoring and evaluation of social work services to the criminal courts and their impact on sentencing outcomes.

Jean Hine holds a joint appointment as Research and Information Officer for Derbyshire Probation Service and Lecturer in Research Methods at Sheffield University. She has carried out various studies of community service since 1974, including the national study reported on here when she was Senior Research Fellow at the University of Birmingham.

Mike Hough is Professor of Social Policy at South Bank University. Previously he was Deputy Head of the Home Office Research and Planning Unit. He has published widely on policing, the British Crime Survey, and community penalties.

Adrian James is Senior Lecturer in Applied Social Studies in the Centre for Criminology and Criminal Justice at the University of Hull. prior to this he was a Senior Probation Officer. He has been substantially involved in research into various aspects of the work of the probation service, and the criminal justice system generally.

Martin Knapp is a health and social care economist whose research, teaching and consultancy activities range across a number of subject areas, both in the UK and elsewhere. His current research is mainly concentrated on mental health services, the developing mixed economies of health and social care (particularly in relation to community care), pharmaceutical products and the voluntary (non-profit) sector. He holds two professorial appointments: he is Professorial Fellow and (Site) Director of the Personal Social Services Research Unit at the London School of Economic and Political Science; and he is also Professor of Health Economics in the Faculty of Medicine, University of London, and Director of the Centre for the Economics of Mental Health at the Institute of Psychiatry. He has degrees in economics and pure mathematics (BA), econometrics (Msc) and social policy (PhD). He has published widely, including 11 books, ll short monographs, 1009 chapters contributed to edited collections, almost 100 peer-review journal articles and 60 other articles. He was co-editor of *Voluntas* for four years, and is a member of a number of editorial boards. He is a regular speaker at UK and international conferences on health care and policy, social services, community care, psychiatry and the voluntary sector.

Charles Lloyd is currently Principal Research Officer in the Home Office Central Drugs Prevention Unit where he is responsible for commissioning research into drug prevention initiatives. He previously worked in the Home Office Research and Planning Unit carrying out research into community penalties and has published many Home Office reports on this topic.

George Mair is Professor of Criminal Justice at Liverpool John Moores University. Prior to this he was for many years a Principal Research Officer in the Home Office Research and Planning Unit where he was responsible for research into community penalties. He is the author of many reports and articles on the work of the probation service and on criminal justice policy. He is currently Executive Secretary of the British Society of Criminology.

Gill McIvor is a Reader in the Social Work Research Centre at Stirling University. She has conducted research into community service, bail information, offender accommodation, probation and throughcare. She is author of *Sentenced to Serve: The Operation and Impact of Community*

Service by Offenders (Avebury, 1992), co-author of *Evaluating Social Work Effectiveness* (Open University Press, 1992) and *Bail Services in Scotland* (Avebury, 1996) and editor of *Working with Offenders: Research Highlights in Social Work 26* (Jessica Kingsley, 1995).

Ann Netten is an Assistant Director at the Personal Social Services Research Unit, University of Kent at Canterbury. She worked in local authority social services before joining the Unit in 1987. Much of her work has focused on costing, covering such diverse areas as health and social services, informal health care and the criminal justice system. Her other interests include care of older people, particularly environmental aspects of residential care and developing theoretical approaches to the evaluation of community care.

Ray Pawson is a Senior Lecturer in Sociology at the University of Leeds. He is the author of *A Measure for Measures: A Manifesto for Empirical Sociology,* (Routledge, 1989), and (with N. Tilley) *Realistic Evaluation* (Sage, forthcoming). He is president of the Research Committee on Methodology of the International Sociological Association and the UK director of the International Forum for the Study of Education in Penal Systems.

Peter Raynor is Professor of Applied Social Studies in the University of Wales, Swansea. A former probation officer, he has published widely on probation topics and on the effectiveness of community services. He was supported by the Nuffield Foundation during the preparation of his chapter.

Bryan Williams is Professor of Social Work at the University of Dundee. His research interests lie in the field of social work and criminal justice, and he has been involved in a number of Government-funded research projects and served on several national commissions and investigative committees.

Introduction

Around the middle of the 1980s, efficiency, effectiveness, economy, value for money, relatively suddenly became key words for the criminal justice agencies. This is not to suggest that such concepts had been ignored before this time or that they did not impinge upon the work of other public sector agencies, but by the second half of the eighties the police, the prison service and the probation service were having to try to come to terms with increased pressure from government for results and, at the same time, increasing budgetary restrictions. All too often, value for money and economy simply meant a cut in resources; and efficiency and effectiveness were rarely differentiated from each other clearly. Studies by the Audit Commission, Financial Management Initiatives, and the introduction of performance indicators are all manifestations of the pressures faced by the criminal justice agencies.

For a time, the probation service seemed to be getting off relatively lightly. Although the publication of the Statement of National Objectives and Priorities (SNOP; Home Office, 1984) was greeted with shock, looking back it is a surprisingly innocuous document. While financial imperatives were beginning to be felt towards the end of the eighties, the service was encouraged by the suggestion of John Patten when, as a Home Office minister, he talked of the service moving centre-stage in the criminal justice drama. The 1991 Criminal Justice Act held out promise for the service and more resources were to be made available to meet the extra demands of the combination order and supervision of prisoners on automatic conditional release. By 1995, probation was reeling under what it saw as relentless attacks by government; cash limits had been imposed, budgets were being cut, the Green Paper *Strengthening Punishment in the Community* (Home Office, 1995) and the White Paper *Protecting the Public* (Home Office, 1996) were seen as threatening, and training was scrapped.

There is a sense in which effectiveness was never a key issue for the probation service until the 1990s. If Nothing Works suggested that probation was not very good at reducing offending (nor, of course, was any other sentence), then it could at least provide an alternative to custody which would save money and the damaging effects of imprisonment; if it could not do these things, then it might be able to alleviate some of the problems faced by offenders (unemployment, substance abuse, poor accommodation, lack of social skills). The probation service were the good guys of the criminal justice system and, as such, beyond serious criticism. All that has changed; the pressure on the probation service to demonstrate its effectiveness has never been greater - although, at the same time, it might be argued that ideas about what constitutes effectiveness have never been more confused.

As the search for effectiveness became more frenetic, so the use of the term 'evaluation' began to be used more regularly. Evaluation has become a buzz word in the last few years in the same way that 'community' did in the eighties when community policing, community crime prevention, community probation work, and the like suddenly sprang into vogue. Just as community became a term to use in order to show that one understood the issues rather than having inherent meaning, so evaluation shows signs of moving in the same direction. It is used more and more by those who, five or ten years ago, would have talked of research; it is used as a synonym for research and as a key to unlock the doors to funding.

The origins of this book lie in my increasing unease about the way in which these two terms - evaluation and effectiveness - were being bandied about without any real consideration for their meaning in the area of community penalties (it should go without saying that these two terms are just as significant for the other criminal justice agencies). The starting-point for the book was two-fold: that evaluation was not the same as research; and that effectiveness involved more than a simplistic reliance upon reconviction rates.

It is not the aim of the book to provide definitive answers to what evaluation is and precisely what effectiveness consists of; the aim is to open up the debate around these two concepts. Evaluation is, I would argue, different from research in its pure form - although it may be difficult to see any differences in practice between the two. There is no doubt that research can be evaluative, and that an evaluation study will include some (if not wholly consist of) research. But evaluation implies some form of assessment of success or failure, some kind of measure of how well or how badly a programme or initiative is meeting its objectives; in other words, evaluation has to do with effectiveness. Evaluation is also connected with the policy process and with 'politics' in a much more intimate fashion than research.

Effectiveness, too, is a complicated issue. Reconviction rates have many limitations which restrict their use as a simple measure of the effectiveness of a court sentence, yet this is precisely how they have been used for many years. This problem raises various questions: can reconviction rates be improved as a measure of effectiveness; can other measures of effectiveness be developed; and, if so, can these be combined in any meaningful way to provide an overall measure of the effectiveness of a sentence ? These are the kind of topics covered by the contributors to this book, both explicitly and implicitly.

But evaluation and effectiveness are not just subjects which are important in themselves; they are relevant to other debates which are currently taking place around community penalties. The 'Nothing Works' debate, for example, has - after years of stagnation - flared into life again with the discovery of meta-analysis. Although relatively few meta-analyses have been carried out so far into the impact of community penalties the effects of these studies have been out of all proportion to their results. For the most part, meta-analysis shows that rehabilitative treatment in the community (however defined) leads to reduced recidivism - and this is a useful advance, but to then go on to make further claims is not helpful. Meta-analysis is not the clear-cut statistical technique which its criminological practitioners often assume it to be (see Losel (1993) and Mair and Copas (forthcoming) for critical accounts). In addition, meta-analysis:

> ..cannot tell us precisely what kind of treatment should be used, when it should be used, in what doses, with what offenders, or within what programmes. Nor does it tell us about the kinds of structures, the kinds of staff required, or the resources necessary to deliver effective programs...Where meta-analysis can be useful is in *suggesting* what appear to be the most promising ways to move forward; it certainly does not offer cast-iron recipes for successful treatment programs. (Mair, 1995)

From this perspective, evaluating the effectiveness of community penalties becomes vital. If good, carefully planned evaluations are not carried out and measures of effectiveness are not well-defined, then we could easily slip back to the negativity of the 'Nothing Works' era.

There is considerable confusion about performance indicators and measures of effectiveness (this is easily seen in the Key Performance Indicators which have been developed for the probation service). It is all too easy to slide from the idea of indicators of performance which are precisely that, to measures of effectiveness which are a different thing altogether. Performance indicators are a means to an end, not an end in themselves; they require careful interpretation; and they do not necessarily show how effectively an organisation is performing. Effectiveness measures are a more complex animal; they will require more work to produce than performance indicators but they should tell you considerably more about an organisation. More work is needed to differentiate between these two concepts.

Evaluating the effectiveness of community penalties can run into two specific 'political' problems: the desire of stakeholders (in this case, the Home Office and the probation service) for quick, easy answers; and fear of the results of evaluation. In the first case, it is obvious that quick, easy answers would be preferable - unfortunately, these are hard to come by. One of the few lessons which can be drawn from the many studies of the outcomes of probation or community service which have been carried out since the end of the Second World War, is that simple answers do not emerge. Dealing with offenders in the community is a difficult and complex task; in working with offenders, probation officers try to grapple with a variety of social problems which cannot be easily resolved, nor is the relationship between such problems and offending clearly defined. Fashions in supervision come and go; research agendas are short-term; researchers can be fickle in their interests. All of these things militate against finding a simple solution to offending. To begin to get a serious grip on the effectiveness of community penalties, researchers must be given time and a simple solution should not be expected.

As for fear of the results of evaluation, this is entirely understandable. If an organisation or individual is to be evaluated in terms of how successful he/she/it is, one will want to be seen to be successful and be apprehensive about the effects if seen to be a failure. If performance pay is involved (or cash limits), the pressures become even greater. And if you feel that the government is gunning for you (and at the time of writing - March 1996 - this is the case for the probation service), the situation is worse. While the probation service generally pays lip service to evaluation, it is all too often ambivalent about the results. The desire to be seen in the best possible light, to make exaggerated claims for projects, and to become defensive about work make evaluations difficult. There is no easy solution to this problem; the pressure for results is not going to go away. The best that might be done is to defuse fear of failure as far as possible: it is important to get across that while many exciting initiatives fail, the key is to find out the reasons for failure, try to ensure that these are not repeated and start again.

The essays in this collection cover many of the issues sketched out in the preceding pages. The first three set the scene in a fairly general way. Gill McIvor summarises the history of evaluative research into probation over the last 30 years, pointing to some of the key issues involved in such research. She notes the growing significance of meta-analysis in this area, but also emphasises the importance of programme content (which is all too often ignored by researchers) and - closely related to this - programme integrity. The fact that different community penalties have different aims and objectives, and that these will also differ for the various individuals/agencies involved, makes the evaluation of effectiveness a complex task. Practitioners in particular need to be much more aware of evaluation and effectiveness and what they mean. She also points to some areas for future research.

Peter Raynor also sums up the recent history of evaluative research into probation, but he links this with the major shifts which have taken place in probation thinking in the past 30 years: primarily with probation as rehabilitative treatment, and probation as diversion. He shows how such views of probation have coloured the research which has been carried out - different conceptions of probation lead to different criteria for effectiveness. Fragmented, partial studies have slowly begun to give way to more inclusive studies which, although more complex, are closer to the realities of probation work. He sets out various considerations which might improve future evaluative studies.

George Mair, Charles Lloyd and Mike Hough deconstruct reconviction rates. They argue that although reconviction rates are usually seen as the sole measure of effectiveness of court sentences and taken for granted as such, they are in fact a complex and problematic measure. They describe the various limitations associated with reconviction rates, not in order to demolish them but in an effort to encourage a more appropriate and sophisticated use of them.

The next five chapters describe examples of research in action which tried to grapple with issues of evaluation and effectiveness. Adrian James and Keith Bottomley describe the problems encountered in trying to assess the impact of the 'Tackling Offending' initiative - in many ways a rather diffuse and nebulous policy initiative. There are always difficulties in relating process findings to outcomes, but in a study like 'Tackling Offending' these were especially problematic. Matters were further complicated by the fact that the Home Office was unclear about criteria for the success or failure of the initiative. The authors argue for a much more detailed examination of the relationship between process and outcome evaluation.

George Mair discusses the intensive probation initiative launched by the Home Office in the late 80s (a partner of 'Tackling Offending'). He shows how the various background factors which led to intensive probation ruled out using a simple research design which focused on reconviction rates. A process and outcome evaluation of the initiative were carried out, with the outcome evaluation considering several different measures of success. The key findings of the study are described, and the advantages and drawbacks of the methodology used are set out.

Bryan Williams and Anne Creamer describe the evaluation of four experimental probation schemes in Scotland. Reconviction rates were eschewed as a measure of effectiveness; instead, diversion from custody was the outcome measure used, and the research orientation was action research. While overall the four schemes achieved their objectives, the ways in which these were achieved differed from scheme to scheme, so that to talk of the initiatives in a global sense would be misleading (cf. intensive probation schemes). The significance of factors other than the probation initiatives themselves in leading to reductions in the use of custody is emphasised.

Jean Hine reflects on a study of community service, a sentence which has always been perceived - indeed celebrated - for its ability to be all things to all people. She describes how what seemed to be even the most simple concepts, such as a community service scheme, were capable of various definitions. And such varying definitions not only had implications for the way in which research was carried out, but also were closely related to the effectiveness of community service.

We often assume that they order these things better in the USA, but as Todd Clear demonstrates this is not always the case. Intensive probation (IP) has been perhaps the major development in probation in the USA during the past ten years, but this is not because of its ability to fulfil its stated goals. Professor Clear argues that the failures of intensive probation lie in the socio-political context in which it was developed and implemented. The 'politics' of IP are crucial to an understanding of its aims and objectives; the effectiveness of IP should not necessarily be judged according to its ability to achieve its stated goals. Rather more covert goals need to be examined.

The final two chapters look forward. Martin Knapp and Ann Netten focus on evaluating the cost and cost-effectiveness of community penalties, an aspect of evaluative research which is often ignored completely or carried out in a very simplistic fashion. They set out a framework which provides basic principles for research into cost-effectiveness, and describe various examples of such research. They also speculate on why so little research has been carried out into the economics of criminal justice issues. Finally, Ray Pawson deplores the confused state of affairs in evaluating community penalties and states the case for a different approach to evaluation based on scientific realism. He shows the failings of the classic quasi-experimental approach to evaluation and describes in some detail a research project being carried out in Simon Fraser University in Canada which follows a scientific realist design. The potential advantages of following a scientific realist methodology for evaluating the effectiveness of community penalties make a fitting end to this book. Whether or not one agrees with the Pawson approach, it is to be hoped that the papers in this collection will lead to better evaluations which will in turn lead to more effective community penalties.

References

Home Office (1984), *Probation Service in England and Wales: Statement of National Objectives and Priorities*, Home Office, London.

Home Office (1995), *Strengthening Punishment in the Community*, Cm 2780, HMSO, London.

Home Office (1996), *Protecting the Public: the government's strategy on crime in England and Wales*, Cm 3190, HMSO, London.

Losel, F. (1993), 'The effectiveness of treatment in institutional and community settings', *Criminal Behaviour and Mental Health*, 3, 416-437.

Mair, G. (1995), 'Evaluating the impact of community penalties', *University of Chicago Law School Roundtable*, 2, 455-474.

Mair, G. and Copas, J. (forthcoming), 'Nothing works and what works - meta-analysis ?'.

1 Evaluative research in probation: progress and prospects

Gill McIvor

Introduction

In a political climate which asserts that 'prison works', that advocates the use of tougher penalties for a growing range of offences and offenders and which aims to undermine the social work base of probation practice (Nellis, 1996), coupled with increased public concern about crime, probation services in England and Wales are under greater pressure than ever before to demonstrate their effectiveness in the supervision of offenders in the community.

In Scotland, too, where the supervision of offenders subject to a range of court disposals or following release from custody remains the responsibility of the local authority social work departments (despite the introduction in 1991 of 100 per cent central government funding of social work services to the criminal justice system (Social Work Services Group, 1991)) there are signs of change. While there is, as yet, no clear indication that the Scottish Office has retreated significantly from its commitment, articulated in 1988 by the then Secretary of State for Scotland (Rifkind, 1989), to encourage the courts to make appropriate use of community based social work disposals, such as probation and community service, recent proposals by the current Scottish Secretary to reduce substantially the amount of remission on prison sentences and to toughen community service orders clearly herald a hardening attitude on the part of policy makers towards those who fall foul of the law.

Across Britain, therefore, those with a statutory responsibility for supervising offenders in the community face the challenge of doing so while being seen to provide the level of public protection that society and politicians appear to demand. Against this backdrop the present chapter examines the progress that has been made in the evaluation of community penalties and considers the shape and direction that future evaluative research should take if it is to inform the development of effective probation practice.

In search of effectiveness

In the 1960s in both Britain and North America criminal justice was characterised by penological optimism allied to the rehabilitative ideal: a belief in the potential to reform offenders through their exposure to a range of therapeutic 'treatments'. This was reflected in Britain in the existence of borstal training, in the introduction of the parole system and in the increasing range of responsibilities accorded to the probation service. The 1970s, by contrast, could be said to be characterised by penological gloom accompanied by a retreat from rehabilitation as a major goal of criminal justice. Thus, in North America there was witnessed a shift towards retributive sentencing based upon notions of deservedness or just desert (Doob and Brodeur, 1989) and an increased emphasis, fuelled by concern about the labelling effect of formal processing, upon the diversion of offenders at various points in the criminal justice process. In Britain, probation officers were encouraged to abandon traditional models of supervision and to adopt instead a 'non-treatment paradigm' (Bottoms and McWilliams, 1979) with, as one of its central theses, the diversion of offenders from custody. Further justification for the adoption by probation services of diversion from custody as a key objective was provided in 1984 when the Home Office issued its Statement of National Objectives and Priorities (SNOP) for the probation service (Home Office, 1984) which identified diversion as a central probation service task. A shift in practice from individual change to system change (or, put another way, from rehabilitation to diversion and gatekeeping) was, perhaps, most clearly evident in the 'new orthodoxy' of juvenile justice in England and Wales during the 1980s (Blagg and Smith, 1989; Pratt, 1987).

It is now generally agreed that a number of factors contributed to the demise of the rehabilitative ideal (Cullen and Gendreau, 1989; McIvor, 1990; Mair, 1991) not least of which was the publication in the 1970s of reviews of the offender treatment literature (e.g. Brody, 1976; Greenberg, 1977; Robison and Smith, 1971) in which the authors were unable to identify approaches which had a consistently positive impact upon recidivism. The most influential of these reviews was undoubtedly the one conducted by Martinson and his colleagues (Lipton et al., 1975; Martinson, 1974) which was widely interpreted as supporting the conclusion that 'nothing works'. Martinson's analysis did not go unchallenged. Palmer (1975), for instance, argued that Martinson had applied overly rigid criteria when judging the effectiveness of different categories of interventions and had failed to take account of the possibility of differential treatment effects which could serve to obscure the fact that some interventions were effective with some offenders. Nevertheless, the more simplistic and unjustified conclusion that nothing works gained widespread support, this being attributed by Cullen and Gendreau (1989) less to the strength of intellectual argument presented than to the fact that it appeared in a social and political climate that was receptive to its message.

Despite being 'an emperor which has been scantily clothed' (Mair, 1991, p. 7) a firm belief by academics and practitioners in the ineffectiveness of any rehabilitative efforts with respect to the reduction of recidivism among offenders persisted for almost two decades. By the beginning of the 1990s, however, several more contemporary literature reviews had been conducted which warranted more positive, albeit still necessarily tentative, conclusions being reached regarding the potential effectiveness of different methods of intervention (Gendreau and Ross, 1979, 1987; Genevie et al., 1986; McIvor, 1990). Indeed, even Martinson himself (who had never, in fact, made such a bald assertion as nothing works) was led to conclude that some interventions could produce meaningful reductions in offending behaviour (Martinson, 1979; Martinson and Wilks, 1977).

The technique of meta-analysis, which was developed by Glass et al. (1981) as a means of eliminating subjectivity and bias in the review and integration of research findings, has recently been applied to the offender treatment literature (e.g. Garrett, 1985; Andrews et al., 1990; Lipsey, 1990). Meta-analysis entails the pooling of data across a number of studies to compute the overall size of the effect achieved by a given method of intervention. It thereby purports to circumvent the difficulties of achieving statistically significant differences with small samples. Advocates of the technique argue that by measuring the size of effects obtained across several studies, and not simply whether an effect has occurred or not, meta-analysis provides a more realistic and accurate assessment of the relative effectiveness of different methods of intervention. Others, however (e.g. Mair, 1994) have been more critical in their appraisal, pointing out, for example, that crude categorisations have been made of complex outcome measures; that the results of meta-analyses are influenced by the statistic chosen; that the choice of studies to include still entails an element of subjectivity; and that different studies may have been grouped together on the basis that they represent similar approaches which are widely different in practice. As Losel (1995, p.81) concludes:

Despite efforts to be systematic and objective, meta-analyses contain more or less subjective categorisations and decisions on the choice of methods. Although these can be tested, we are still basically confronted with the same problems of measurement that we find in primary studies.

These and other criticisms aside, meta-analyses have generally (but see Whitehead and Lab, 1989) produced conclusions comparable to those derived from the more recent qualitative or narrative reviews. Thus traditional casework, psychotherapies and other unfocused approaches have been largely discredited, as have those approaches which are premised upon a deterrent rationale, which aim to punish but not to help. Instead, it is suggested, intervention should be structured and focused, it should be targeted at offenders who present a higher risk of recidivism, it should address both offending behaviour and underlying criminogenic needs, it should be properly implemented and it should be delivered by appropriately trained staff. Community-based interventions appear to be more effective than those which are provided in institutional settings and offence-focused work which adopts behavioural or cognitive behavioural methods appears more consistently than that employing other less structured methods to impact positively upon recidivism. There is, therefore, growing evidence that appropriately targeted, focused, structured and implemented programmes of supervision can work with at least some offenders. Future research needs to focus upon identifying more precisely what it is that works, why it works, who it works with and under what conditions (Mair, 1991; Palmer, 1992)

Developments in evaluative research

The United States Panel on Research on Rehabilitative Techniques (Sechrest et al., 1979) supported the broad conclusions reached by Martinson and his colleagues, suggesting, indeed, that if anything they had been overly lenient in their assessment of methodology and statistical analysis in respect of individual studies. They concluded that the 'entire body of research appears to justify only the conclusion that we do not know of any program or method of rehabilitation that could be guaranteed to reduce the criminal activity of released prisoners' (p.3) but nevertheless acknowledged the existence of differential treatment effects. More significantly, however, they stressed that much of the research reviewed by Martinson had been lacking in methodological rigour, leading them to observe (p.8) that:

When it is asserted that 'nothing works', the Panel is uncertain as to just what has ever been given a fair trial. If we are to arrive at sound conclusions about the prospects for rehabilitation, future research on offender rehabilitation must pay far more attention to issues of strength and integrity of treatments along with the adequacy of experimental designs.

Rezmovic (1979) has similarly argued that weak experimental designs and lax methodologies are among the strongest impediments to ascertaining which types of intervention are most effective. However, as Losel (1995) has shown, evidence regarding the impact of design quality on the size of treatment effects in meta-analyses is equivocal and appears to be influenced by the method of classification employed. Whilst there is little doubt that a well controlled experimental design can reduce the likelihood of interpretive problems of the type which may occur with the use of comparison groups or with a single group pre- post-test design, random allocation can rarely be achieved in practice and high non-random drop-out rates may cause the original experimental design to collapse (Clark and Cornish, 1972; Farrington, 1983). Traditional experimental or quasi-experimental designs may, moreover, be limited in their utility since they are often unable to differentiate between the relative contributions of different components of complex interventions to the outcomes that are observed. In this respect, more is likely to be learned from research designs - such as the cross-institutional design - which allow for the delineation of programme variables and the measurement of their effects on outcome, though their complexity should not be underestimated (Fuller, 1987; Cheetham et al., 1992).

In their reference to the strength and integrity of treatments, Sechrest et al. (1979) were alluding to a shortcoming which has been characteristic of much evaluative research in this field. In the majority of the published research literature little, if any, attention has been devoted to describing the intervention that is the subject of scrutiny, let alone commenting upon the extent to which it had been implemented as planned. The consequences of such lack of attention to programme content are, perhaps, self evident. It may, for example, result in interventions which are quite dissimilar being lumped together as homogenous categories in meta-analysis and qualitative reviews. It prevents replication of the intervention and its evaluation in other sites. And it may result in the rejection of intervention as ineffective when, if it had been properly implemented, a positive impact upon recidivism may have been achieved.

Greater attention is now being paid to the concept of programme integrity: the congruence between the implementation of a programme in practice and its intended implementation in terms of theory and design.

Hollin (1995, p. 196) has argued that effective programmes of intervention aimed at reducing recidivism have high levels of programme integrity which is dependent upon 'sound management, tight designs and skilled practitioners'. Hollin further suggests that threats to programme integrity occur when practitioners, for whatever reasons, depart from the intended objectives or content of the intervention. A further threat, which relates less directly to the content and delivery of a programme, occurs as a consequence of attrition or non-attandance of participants. It is hardly surprising, for example, that Ostrom et al. (1971) found no evidence of a lasting impact upon re-offending of an offence groupwork programme for young probationers when only 12 of the 19 participants attended three or more of the seven groupwork sessions which were provided.

Another criticism of the offender treatment literature has centred upon the use of recidivism as the (often only) benchmark against which the effectiveness of community penalties is assessed (McIvor, 1990; Mair, 1991; Raynor, 1995). Different studies, for instance, have adopted varying definitions of recidivism ranging from re-arrest to imprisonment for further offences and have adopted follow-up periods of differing lengths. In Britain reconviction has more consistently been adopted as the measure of recidivism. But reconviction cannot be assumed to provide an accurate estimate of further offending: not all of those who have re-offended will have been detected, arrested, charged and convicted while, conversely, some apparent reconvictions (or 'pseudo-convictions') may pertain to offences committed prior to the date from which reconviction is being measured as a consequence of delays in the processing of offenders through the criminal justice system. Furthermore, as a result of biases within the criminal justice system, some categories of offenders may be more likely to fall under suspicion, to be arrested and to be convicted. In comparing the effect of imprisonment with that of community penalties, some studies have measured reconviction from the point of sentence while others have taken the initial point of the follow-up period as the date (actual or estimated) of the prisoner's release (see Lloyd et al. 1994).

Clearly, then, there has been little consensus as to how, in terms of recidivism, the effects of different penalties or of different programmes of intervention should be assessed. This, as Mair (1994) has argued, is particularly problematic when a large number of studies are subjected to meta-analysis with little regard to the definition of recidivism or the length of follow-up period adopted. What is equally clear, however, is that more sophisticated and careful analyses of recidivism are required. The use of binary measures - such as whether or not an individual has been reconvicted within a given period - may mask subtle but nonetheless significant changes in the frequency or seriousness of offending. In an examination of reconviction following community service in Scotland (McIvor, 1992) which was aimed at determining whether there was an association between offenders' experiences of community service and their subsequent reconviction, attention was paid to the rate, frequency and nature of reconviction in the three years following the imposition of an order. The rate of reconviction was found to differ slightly, but not significantly, between the two groups of offenders concerned (those who had reported their experience of CS as having been rewarding and those who had not considered it worthwhile) but the former group were reconvicted less often and fewer were reconvicted of property offences even though they were just as likely to have previous convictions for property offences or to have been sentenced to community service for this type of offence. Other studies which have examined the types of offences for which offenders subject to supervision have been reconvicted have similarly found that the most marked impact of probation programmes appears to be upon the commission of property offences (Roberts, 1989; Raynor and Vanstone, 1994). This is understandable since offences of this type are more likely than others, such as violent offences, to have an element of prior planning or premeditation: offence-focused probation programmes usually aim to engage offenders in an exploration of their offending behaviour with a view to influencing in a positive direction the choices they make.

A problem may still remain, however, in attributing apparent effects of intervention to the intervention itself rather than to other extraneous factors. Thus, according to Waldo and Griswold (1979), recidivism studies only permit conclusions to be reached about the extent to which a particular intervention was unsuccessful. Since other factors may affect recidivism (such as increased maturity, getting a job, finding a partner and so on) it is fallacious, so the argument goes, to conclude that a reduction in recidivism is indicative of rehabilitative success. For this reason, evaluative studies which seek to draw upon a range of outcome measures and which adopt a range of research techniques are likely to offer greater illuminative and explanatory potential. In a recent, and as yet unpublished, study of probation supervision in Scotland, for example, interviews were conducted with probationers who had recently completed their orders or who had recently been breached to explore their perceptions of their risk of recidivism, the extent to which they perceived that risk to have changed since being placed on probation and, where relevant, the relative contribution played by probation supervision and by other factors to any reduction in risk. Similar issues were explored with social workers in individual cases, permitting a comparison to be made of the views of probationers and of supervising officers. The data thus generated offer greater insights into the relative significance of intervention and of other factors, both positive and negative, to the absence or existence of continued offending by probationers.

Drawing upon a range of outcome measures is also necessary since different sentences and different programmes of intervention will have a range of primary and secondary objectives which may include, but which will also extend beyond, the reduction or cessation of offending behaviour. To focus upon recidivism to the exclusion of other outcome measures is to submit interventions to an unfair test. Indeed, it is questionable whether recidivism is an appropriate outcome measure for some sentences, such as community service, which do not have the reduction of recidivism as a primary objective. Why should we be concerned, then, if community service appears to be no more effective than prison in this respect? (Lloyd et al., 1994) The danger, of course, is that a pre-occupation with recidivism deflects attention from the other objectives of sentences such as, in the case of community service, their ability to divert appropriate offenders from custody, their cost effectiveness or the benefits they can bestow upon the community or upon the offenders themselves.

As Mair (1991) points out, in terms of their objectives, community penalties may share some commonalities, but so do they differ in significant respects. Furthermore, the relative importance which is attached to the different objectives by different stakeholders (such as sentencers, policy makers, managers, practitioners, victims and offenders) will vary. While offenders may attach considerable significance to the avoidance of a custodial sentence, community protection may feature more highly on the agenda of sentencers and victims, while policy makers and managers may more than other groups be concerned that the service is cost effective. To address the interests of these various audiences requires a pluralistic approach to evaluation in which a range of primary and secondary objectives (some of which may be specific to a particular programme or individual offender) can be identified and addressed.

The programme of research into the operation and impact of community service in Scotland (McIvor, 1992) exemplifies an approach to evaluation in which the effectiveness of a sentencing option is assessed in relation to a range of primary and secondary objectives. Thus a series of inter-related studies were conducted which examined the impact of operational practice upon the completion of orders; offenders' experiences and views of undertaking unpaid work; the experiences of individuals and agencies who had benefited from community service work; sentencers' perceptions of community service (Carnie, 1990); and the comparative costs of community service and alternative custodial sentences (Knapp et al., 1992). As previously discussed, a further element of the research programme was an examination of reconviction among offenders who had been sentenced to community service, not with the aim of comparing the performance of community service with other sentences in this respect (since community service is not an expressly rehabilitative penalty and should not, therefore, be assessed in these terms), but to examine whether particular features of the community service experience might be associated with secondary benefits in the shape of reductions in recidivism following completion of an order.

The Home Office study of intensive probation programmes in England and Wales (see Mair, this volume; also Raynor, 1988) likewise typifies such a pluralistic approach to the evaluation of probation practice which focused upon both process and outcomes. An emphasis upon process - pursued through detailed case studies of three schemes - was justified by the experimental nature of the initiative in which variations in practice were encouraged and could be captured by an evaluation of this type. Consistent with the primary objectives of intensive probation, outcome measures included: reconviction rates (as variously defined), the ability of intensive probation to divert offenders from custody; the views of sentencers; the views of offenders who participated in the schemes; and the financial costs.

Just as examples can now be found of research which has adopted a more holistic approach to the evaluation of community penalties, so too can studies which have aimed to investigate the manner and context in which initiatives have been developed, the factors which have prevented initiatives from being more successful and those which have contributed to their success. Programme integrity - the extent to which the delivery of a programme corresponds to what was actually planned - is only one aspect of a process evaluation which will look more broadly at both internal and external variables which have had some bearing upon an initiative's success. The purpose of a process evaluation has been described by Mair et al (1994, p.8) as follows:

> A process evaluation will show how an initiative was devised in the first place and the reasons for this; it will show how it was put into practice and whether or not this differed from the blueprint; it will investigate developments over time and attempt to demonstrate why subsequent changes took place. By doing these things, a process evaluation provides the context within which outcomes can be fully interpreted.

The latter point is particularly significant (Cheetham et al, 1992). As Clark and Cornish (1972, p.19) have argued 'knowing that something has made a difference is very little use unless it can be identified'. A similar point is made by Smith (1987, p.406) when he asserts that 'research which is exclusively concerned with outcomes rather than process suffers from the serious limitation that it is impossible to tell what the outcomes were outcomes of'. The relevance of process evaluation in the context of experimental initiatives is now being recognised both by academics and by the funders of research. The Home Office study of intensive probation is one such example. Two others can be found in recent studies funded by the Scottish Office both of which focused upon the development of intervention programmes for sex offenders with a view to better informing the development of similar initiatives. The first study (McIvor et al., forthcoming) centred upon an innovative prison-based groupwork programme for sex offenders which had been introduced in a long term prison housing vulnerable prisoners. Through interviews with staff throughout the prison (including those who were closely involved in the development and delivery of the programme and those who were less directly affected by its introduction) and with prisoners (including programme participants, other sexual offenders and non-sexual offenders) the research was able to identify those factors which had facilitated the implementation of the programme and those which had prevented it being implemented more effectively. Whilst further outcome research will be necessary to evaluate the impact of the programme upon subsequent recidivism, the process evaluation was able to provide practical pointers for the host institution and for other prisons which were considering the development of a programme of this type. It will also, as Mair et al. (1994) have argued, provide a context within which the longer term outcomes of intervention can be more fully interpreted and understood.

The second study (Buist and Fuller, forthcoming) was similar in purpose though the nature of the programme and, as a consequence, the methods adopted were somewhat different. This research focused upon a community-based project, located within the voluntary sector, which worked on an individual and group basis (the latter being a more recent development) with young people who had sexually abused other children. Again the concern was not with measuring outcomes but with describing the context in which the project was established, the way in which it was developed, the methods employed by project staff and their theoretical rationale and the progress of young people through the project including, in a sub-sample of cases, the detailed programme of work undertaken.

Research of this kind can offer commentary upon the feasibility of innovative initiatives and highlight practical issues which will require attention if similar projects are to be successfully introduced and sustained. In his study of the Afan project, for instance, Raynor (1988) was able to identify features in the operation of the scheme which appeared to have contributed significantly to its effectiveness. These included mechanisms for gatekeeping, effective referrals systems, the development of clear contracts with participants and high levels of client contact, a high level of involvement with the courts, the content of the programme, the skills of staff, management support and the role of the local management committee. Raynor also observed, however, that the impact of the scheme appeared to have declined over time, attributing this to factors such as a reduction in court involvement and a reduction of local representation in the management of the scheme.

Studies of intensive probation projects in the United States have produced broadly similar conclusions regarding the organisational and external factors which are necessary to sustain the survival of innovative projects: clear objectives which meet the needs of the 'customers' and which address a locally identified need; the commitment of staff and their ownerships of the project; clear lines of accountability and effective management support; adequate resources; and support from other agencies or individuals upon whose co-operation the success of the venture depends. As Petersilia (1990, p. 144) has noted, '(u)nless a community recognises or accepts the premise that a change in corrections is needed, is affordable, and does not conflict with its sentiments regarding just punishment, an innovative project has little hope of surviving, much less succeeding'.

Building evaluation into practice - the reflexive practitioner

A much welcomed development of late has been the growing interest of practitioners in developing and promoting effective practice and, more specifically, in evaluating their work with offenders. Whilst it is unreasonable to expect practitioners to undertake detailed and complex analyses of the impact of probation practice upon recidivism, probation officers and social workers are increasingly making use of a variety of methods - such as standardised schedules and feedback questionnaires - to evaluate their work with clients. Several factors appear to underlie this increasing interest in practitioner evaluation. The progress that has been made of late in identifying instances of probation work with offenders which have impacted positively upon recidivism (e.g. Roberts, 1989; Brownlee, 1992) and the identification in more general terms of approaches which may offer some promise in this respect have no doubt rekindled practitioners' interest in effectiveness and in evaluative research. Probation officers and social workers are, in addition, operating in a policy context which increasingly emphasises efficiency, effectiveness and value for money. In the face of finite resources, managers and practitioners are recognising the need to be accountable for the quality and the effectiveness of the services they provide (Finkelstein, 1996). To do so requires the development of monitoring systems which can provide feedback about service performance to facilitate the management of services and ensure that resources are appropriately and efficiently deployed.

Yet monitoring systems alone are not enough. They can provide information about what is happening and alert practitioners and managers to potential problems (with respect, for example, to the targeting of services). To determine the impact of services upon short term outcomes requires that additional measures - such as exit questionnaires, problem checklists and standardised instruments which can assess attitudinal change - are introduced with a view to assessing the extent to which the objectives of supervision (some of which may be specific to individual offenders) have been achieved. Mechanisms for obtaining client feedback have the additional advantage of alerting staff to aspects of service provision which may require attention if the quality of services, their relevance to offenders and their effectiveness are to be improved.

As Mair (1993) has indicated, the development of programmes and initiatives by probation services is often a 'bottom-up' process, driven by the interests and enthusiasm of practitioners rather than being the result of a strategic and co-ordinated approach to service development. In the absence of explicit management support and without some attempt having been made to document the operation and impact of innovative projects or methods of work as a means of convincing others of their worth, their survival is unlikely beyond the initial flurry of enthusiasm. As McGuire (1991, p.50) has argued:

> Numerous, ingenious programmes have been carefully nurtured into existence and steered through to their conclusions, only to disappear - because not one shred of evidence had been gathered about their clientele, their functioning or their effectiveness. Systematic programme planning involves the notion of 'what to evaluate and how' being embedded into the thinking of the staff group from the outset of the enterprise.

Modest mechanisms for monitoring and evaluating practice can readily be integrated by staff into the supervision of offenders in the community. An informed approach to management and service development requires that monitoring and evaluation are recognised by practitioners and by managers as integral components of probation practice. This, in turn, requires the development and maintenance of a 'culture of evaluation' (McIvor, 1995) or a 'culture of curiosity' (Raynor, 1996) in which the importance of evaluation in further refining our understanding of what works in the supervision of offenders and in promoting the development of effective practice is recognised and responded to by staff at all levels of the organisation.

Conclusions

In a political climate which advocates the use of increasingly punitive measures in response to criminal behaviour, arguments in support of more humane and constructive sentencing options are unlikely to be won by exhortation alone. A sound empirical base is required to demonstrate the potential and the limitations of community penalties and to further advance our understanding, which is still embryonic, of what works, with which offenders and under which conditions, in reducing offending behaviour. In addition to a general need for further evaluative research which can underpin future probation policy and practice, specific aspects of probation work are worthy of more detailed scrutiny than has hitherto been the case. Much of the research which has focused upon women in the criminal justice system, for example, has concentrated upon the differential treatment of male and female offenders by the courts - including the ways in which probation officers might, through their pre-sentence report practice, contribute to this - or their experiences of imprisonment. Barker's (1993) study of community service is one of the few pieces of research which has addressed directly womens' experiences of community penalties (and Barker herself acknowledges that the picture painted by their accounts may be unduly positive because women whose orders were breached were not included in the sample). Less still is known of women's experiences of probation supervision and, in particular, whether any broad principles that might be extracted from the effectiveness literature are equally applicable to the development of effective probation practice with women offenders. A similar argument can equally be advanced with respect to the issue of race.

More research activity also needs to be directed towards the evaluation of mainstream probation work. As Raynor (1995) has pointed out, the majority of evaluative research in the field of probation in recent years has concentrated upon innovative or specialist projects. Whilst research of this kind has made a significant contribution to our understanding of which approaches to working with offenders in the community might be more likely to yield positive results, the projects concerned do not typify the majority of probation practice and the findings derived from them shed little light on what might realistically be achieved through the mainstream supervision of offenders in the community and in the absence of the high levels of enthusiasm and commitment and the more generous staffing ratios which often characterise 'special' projects.

Over the past few years the evaluation of community penalties has advanced beyond a pre-occupation with recidivism rates with their inherent limitations as the sole criteria of success. Evaluative research in Britain is now characterised by a concern with more sophisticated and meaningful analyses of recidivism and by a more broad-ranging focus in which the ability of community penalties to achieve a range of policy and practice objectives is assessed. The importance of process evaluation is also being increasingly recognised as a means of providing a context in which the outcomes of intervention might be better understood. The evaluation of community penalties requires methodological pluralism which is characterised by pragmatism, imagination, inventiveness and discipline through the rigorous application, combination and adaptation of existing research methods. As Cheetham et al. (1992, pp.6-7) have argued, what is required, in short, is:

> ....an approach to evaluative research which takes account of the complexities of the context, tasks and methods of social work and which produces studies that are seen as comprehensible and relevant to the different parties involved with it...The price and promise about such research is that it can raise as many questions as it answers...In the world of social work there are few simple certainties'.

References

Andrews, D.A., Zinger, I., Hoge, R.D., Bonta, J., Gendreau, P. and Cullen, F.T. (1990), 'Does correctional treatment work? A clinically relevant and psychologically informed meta-analysis', *Criminology*, *28*, 369-404.

Barker, M. (1993), *Community Service for Women Offenders*, London: Association of Chief Officers of Probation.

Blagg, H. and Smith, D. (1989), *Crime, Penal Policy and Social Work*, Longman, London:

Bottoms, A.E. and McWilliams, W. (1979), 'A non-treatment paradigm for probation practice', *British Journal of Social Work*, *9*, 159-202.

Brody, S. R. (1976), *The Effectiveness of Sentencing: A Review of the Literature*, Home Office Research Study No. 35, HMSO, London:

Brownlee, I.D. (1992), *Leeds Young Adult Offenders Project: A Third Evaluation Report*, National Children's Homes.

Buist, M. and Fuller, R. (forthcoming), *Working with Young People who have Sexually Abused Others: An Evaluative Study of an Innovative Project*, Scottish Office Central Research Unit, Edinburgh.

Carnie, J. (1990), *Sentencers' Perceptions of Community Service by Offenders*, Scottish Office Central Research Unit, Edinburgh.

Cheetham, J., Fuller, R., McIvor, G. and Petch, A. (1992) *Evaluating Social Work Effectiveness*, Open University Press, Milton Keynes.

Clark, R.V.G. and Cornish, D.B. (1972), *The Controlled Trial in Institutional Research: Paradigm or Pitfall for Penal Evaluators*, Home Office Research Study No. 15,: HMSO, London.

Cullen, F.T. and Gendreau, P. (1989), 'The effectiveness of correctional rehabilitation: Reconsidering the 'nothing works' debate', in L. Goodstein and D.L. Mackenzie (Eds.) *The American Prison: Issues in Research and Policy*,: Plenum Press, New York.

Doob, A.N. and Brodeur, J. (1989) 'Rehabilitating the debate on rehabilitation', *Canadian Journal of Criminology, 31*, 179-95.

Farrington, D.P. (1983), 'Randomised experiments on crime and justice', in M. Tonry and N. Morris (eds.) *Crime and Justice: An Annual Review of Research Volume 4*, University of Chicago Press, Chicago.

Finkelstein, E. (1996), 'Values in context: Quality assurance, autonomy and accountability', in T. May and A.A. Vass (eds.) *Working with Offenders: Issues, Contexts and Outcomes*, Sage, London.

Fuller, R. (1987), *The Cross-Institutional Research Design: Paradigm or Pitfall?*, Social Work Research Centre, University of Stirling, Stirling.

Garrett, C.J. (1985), 'Effects of residential treatment on adjudicated delinquents: A meta-analysis', *Journal of Research in Crime and Delinquency, 22*, 287-308.

Gendreau, P. and Ross, R.R. (1979), 'Effective correctional treatment: Bibliotherapy for cynics', *Crime and Delinquency, 25*, 463-89.

Gendreau, P. and Ross, R.R. (1987), 'Revivification of rehabilitation: Evidence from the 1980s', *Justice Quarterly, 4*, 349-407.

Genevie, L. Margolies, E. and Muhlin, G.L. (1986), 'How effective is correctional intervention?', *Social Policy, 16*, 52-7.

Glass, G.V., McGaw, B. and Smith, M.L. (1981), *Meta-analysis in Social Research*, Sage, Beverly Hills.

Greenberg, D.F. (1977), 'The correctional effects of corrections: A survey of evaluations', in D.F. Greenberg (ed.) *Corrections and Punishment*, Sage, Beverly Hills.

Hollin, C.R. (1995), 'The meaning and implications of programme integrity', in J. McGuire (ed.), *What Works: Reducing Reoffending*, Wiley, London.

Home Office (1984), *Probation Service in England and Wales: Statement of National Objectives and Priorities*, Home Office, London.

Lipsey, M.W. (1990), 'Juvenile delinquency treatment: a meta-analytic enquiry into the variability of effects', in T.D. Cook et al. (eds.), *Meta-analysis for Explanation: A Casebook*, Russell Sage Foundation, New York.

Lipton, D., Martinson, R. and Wilks, J. (1975), *Effectiveness of Correctional Treatment: A Survey of Treatment Evaluation Studies*, Praeger, Springfield.

Lloyd, C., Mair, G. and Hough, M. (1994), *Explaining Reconviction Rates: A Critical Analysis*, Home Office Research Study No. 136, HMSO, London.

Losel, F. (1995), 'The efficacy of correctional treatment: A review and synthesis of meta-evaluations', in J. McGuire (ed.), *What Works: Reducing Reoffending*, John Wiley, London.

Mair, G. (1991), 'What works - nothing or everything? Measuring the effectiveness of sentences', *Home Office Research and Statistics Department Research Bulletin No. 30*, HMSO, London.

Mair, G. (1993), *Specialist Activities in Probation: Confusion Worse Confounded?*, paper presented at the British Criminology Conference, University of Wales, Cardiff.

Mair, G. (1994), *Standing at the Crossroads: What Works in Community Penalties*, paper presented at the National Conference for Probation Committee Members, Scarborough.

Mair, G., Lloyd, C., Nee, C. and Sibbitt, R. (1994), *Intensive probation in England and Wales: An evaluation*, Home Office Research Study No. 133, HMSO, London.

Martinson, R. (1974), 'What works?: Questions and answers about prison reform', *The Public Interest*, 23, 22-54.

Martinson, R. (1979), 'New findings, new views: a note of caution regarding sentencing reform', *Hofstra Law Review*, 7, 243-58.

Martinson, R. and Wilks, J. (1977), Save parole supervision, *Federal Probation, 42*, 23-7.

McGuire, J. (1991), 'Things to do to make your programme work', in *What Works: Effective Methods to Reduce Re-Offending (Conference Proceedings)*, Greater Manchester Probation Service, Manchester.

McIvor, G. (1990), *Sanctions for Serious or Persistent Offenders: A Review of the Literature*, Social Work Research Centre, University of Stirling, Stirling.

McIvor, G. (1992), *Sentenced to Serve: The Operation and Impact of Community Service by Offenders*, Avebury, Aldershot.

McIvor, G. (1995), 'Practitioner evaluation in probation', in J. McGuire (ed.), *What Works: Reducing Reoffending*, John Wiley, London.

McIvor, G., Campbell, V., Rowlings, C. and Skinner, K. (forthcoming), *The STOP Programme: The Development and Implementation of Prison-Based Groupwork with Sex Offenders*, Scottish Prison Service Occasional Paper, Edinburgh.

Nellis, M. (1996) 'Probation training: The links with social work', in T. May and A.A. Vass (eds.), *Working with Offenders: Issues, Contexts and Outcomes*, Sage, London.

Ostrom, T.M., Steele, C.M., Rosenblood, L.K. and Mirels, H.L (1971), 'Modification of delinquent behavior', *Journal of Applied Social Psychology, 1*, 118-36.

Palmer, T. (1975), 'Martinson revisited', *Journal of Research in Crime and Delinquency, 12*, 133-52.

Palmer, T. (1992), *The Re-Emergence of Correctional Intervention*, Sage, London.

Petersilia, J. (1990), 'Conditions that permit intensive supervision programs to survive', *Crime and Delinquency, 36*, 126-45.

Pratt, J. (1987), 'A revisionist history of intermediate treatment', *British Journal of Social Work, 17*, 417-36.

Raynor, P. (1988) *Probation as an Alternative to Custody*, Avebury, Aldershot.

Raynor, P. (1995), 'Effectiveness now: a personal and selective overview', in G. McIvor (ed.), *Working with Offenders: Research Highlights in Social Work 26*, Jessica Kingsley, London.

Raynor, P. (1996) 'Evaluating probation: the rehabilitation of effectiveness', in T. May and A.A. Vass (eds.), *Working with Offenders: Issues, Contexts and Outcomes*, Sage, London.

Raynor, P. and Vanstone, M. (1994), *Straight Thinking on Probation - Third Evaluation Report: Reconvictions within 12 months following STOP Orders, custodial sentences and other community sentences,*: Mid Glamorgan Probation Service, Bridgend.

Rezmovic, E.L. (1979), 'Methodological considerations in evaluating correctional effectiveness: Issues and chronic problems', in L. Sechrest et al. (eds.), *The Rehabilitation of Criminal Offenders: Problems and Prospects*, National Academy of Sciences, Washington D.C.

Rifkind, M. (1989), 'Penal policy: The way ahead', *Howard Journal of Criminal Justice, 28*, 81-90.

Roberts, C.H. (1989), *Hereford and Worcester Probation Service Young Offender Project: First Evaluation Report*, Hereford and Worcester Probation Service.

Robison, J. and Smith, S. (1971), 'The effectiveness of correctional programs', *Crime and Delinquency, 17*, 67-80.

Sechrest, L., White, S.O. and Brown, E.D. (1979.), *The Rehabilitation of Criminal Offenders: Problems and Prospects*, National Academy of Sciences, Washington D.C.

Smith, D. (1987), 'The limits of positivism in social work research', *British Journal of Social Work, 17*, 401-16.

Social Work Services Group (1991), *National Objectives and Standards for Social Work Services in the Criminal Justice System*, The Scottish Office, Edinburgh.

Waldo, G.P. and Griswold, D. (1979), 'Issues in the measurement of recidivism', in L. Sechrest et al. (eds.), *The Rehabilitation of Criminal Offenders: Problems and Prospects,* National Academy of Sciences, Washington D.C.

Whitehead, J.T. and Lab, S.P. (1989), 'A meta-analysis of juvenile correctional treatment', *Journal of Research in Crime and Delinquency,* *26,* 276-95.

2 Evaluating probation: a moving target

Peter Raynor

This chapter aims to explore some of the interactions between policy and practice development and evaluative research in probation. During the past twenty years there have been major shifts in both official and professional thinking about the role and function of probation services and about the purposes and aims of probation orders; these have both influenced and been influenced by evaluative research, though never determined by it, and the questions asked by researchers have both reflected and helped to shape the ideas behind official policy. Researchers cannot evaluate a process or activity unless they have some idea of its purposes, and they cannot simply invent these for themselves or the results of their evaluations will be of little practical use; conversely, purposes formed by policy-makers or practitioners need to be informed by ideas about what is in practice feasible or achievable. As moral philosophers put it, 'ought implies can'. It has also been argued that activities with such a long professional and institutional history as probation come to have their own inherent purposes, and that the aims of a social practice become, in effect, part of its definition, not something which can be altered at will by shifts in policy: its purposes and values are expressed by the activity itself and should inform both evaluation and policy development (McWilliams, 1989). If we are optimists, we might see the relationship between policy, practice and research as a continuous dialogue in which all three interact to their mutual benefit; but researchers should also be realists, and at best this is a dialogue in which any of the parties may be suddenly afflicted with deafness.

The history of probation in England and Wales goes back for more than a hundred years, but this chapter is mainly concerned with the last quarter of this history. Even within the relatively brief period of the last twenty five years it is possible to identify at least two and possibly three major transformations in official and professional thinking about probation, each of which has had different effects on the issues investigated by probation researchers and on the nature of the dialogue between research, policy and practice. In addition, the picture has been complicated by other factors such as the location of research inside and outside Government departments, and by current uncertainties about the significance and long-term effects of recent political developments. Like any history this must be a simplified account, and the selection of particular research studies for comment does not mean that there have not been others, nor that others are unimportant; however, I have tried to select those which seem to me to reflect most clearly the changing conceptions of probation during this period.

Rethinking probation at least twice

What, then, have been the major changes in thinking? To summarise a long and complicated story, early British studies of the effects of probation such as Wilkins (1958) and Radzinowicz (1958) were clearly located within what subsequently became known as the 'treatment model': in Radzinowicz's formulation, probation was 'a form of social service preventing further crime by a readjustment of the culprit', and studies were designed to measure whether this readjustment had been successfully achieved. They investigated reconviction, assumed to be a surrogate measure of reoffending. The Home Office Research Unit (as it was then known) undertook a number of ambitious studies of probation and related areas during the late 1960s and early 1970s, including some very complex and sophisticated investigations such as Davies (1974), in a determined search for the effects of probation on recidivism: some of these studies will be discussed further later in the chapter. For the moment, it is sufficient to note that they were concerned with the effects of probation on offenders' behaviour, and took it for granted that this was what probation was about. The professional literature of the time, which intending probation officers read or pretended to read on their training courses, was informed by American models of psychosocial casework (e.g. Monger, 1964; Foren and Bailey, 1968) and dealt uneasily but at length with the apparent contradiction between the voluntary relationship of therapist and client and the court-mandated relationship between probation officer and offender. (The usual solution to this difficulty was that offenders were too immature to understand their real needs and interests as probation officers did, so the relationship was effectively voluntary even if offenders had not volunteered, because they would have done so if they had been mature enough to understand why they should. This argument could be stated much more convincingly by those who believed in it - see Hunt, 1964).

By the end of the 1970s the 'treatment model' was being strongly criticised on a number of empirical and ethical grounds. Empirically, studies of the effectiveness of penal sanctions of all kinds had produced generally discouraging results, and while this was not true of all studies, the general impression that 'nothing works' was reinforced by journalistic summaries (Martinson, 1974) and by the overall conclusions of wide-ranging research reviews (Lipton et al., 1975; Brody, 1976). These findings also gained strength from what were essentially moral or philosophical arguments against 'treatment', such as that it objectified or dehumanised its subjects, or that it rested on unsubstantiated claims of superior professional wisdom (Bottoms and McWilliams, 1979). Legal scholars were increasingly questioning whether unreliable predictions about future behaviour should continue to influence sentencing and argued instead for proportionate 'justice' based on the seriousness of the offence (Hood, 1974; Von Hirsch, 1976). Meanwhile researchers on juvenile justice following the 'treatment'-oriented 1969 Children and Young Persons Act were beginning to document unintended adverse consequences such as increased incarceration following the failure of community-based supervision to prevent further offending (Thorpe et al., 1980). It began to appear that young offenders, like their older counterparts, might actually benefit from proportionate 'tariff' sentencing which did not aim to do them good but would at least avoid the excesses of overambitious compulsory 'treatment'. If the emphasis of the 1970s had been on doing good without much success in demonstrating that good was being done, the 1980s were to be about avoiding harm, in particular by reducing unnecessary incarceration. This seemed a more achievable aim, and one which might commend itself on the grounds of economy even to communities or politicians who were not in sympathy with the underlying humanitarian aim. So began the era of 'alternatives to custody': probation was to be a non-custodial penalty aiming to increase its market share and reduce imprisonment, rather than a 'treatment' aiming to change people.

By the end of the 1980s these principles were well enough accepted to be argued in Green and White papers (Home Office, 1988, 1990a, 1990b) and embodied in the 1991 Criminal Justice Act, which articulated for the first time in legislation a sentencing rationale based on punishment proportionate to the seriousness of the offence. Probation was to be one of a number of 'community sentences' for those whose offences were serious enough to require a significant sanction but not so serious that only a custodial sentence could be justified. The language of 'alternatives to custody' was now discouraged, but the underlying aim was to make community sentences the standard disposal for middle-range offenders, reserving imprisonment for the most serious or those who presented most risk to the public. Although most probation officers disliked the accompanying rhetoric of 'punishment in the community', which was no doubt intended for public consumption rather than for the professional audience, the Act and the accompanying National Standards paradoxically helped to encourage the next significant shift in probation thinking. The expectation of more frequent contact with supervised offenders and of more demanding and meaningful forms of supervision helped to motivate a search for useful content in supervision programmes.

21

This search was significantly assisted by an emerging international tendency to question the received wisdom of the 'nothing works' era. Approaches to supervision programme design based on structured social learning, derived for example from psychological approaches to offending behaviour (McGuire and Priestley, 1985) and from practice in probation day centres (Vanstone, 1993), had already gained some adherents in British probation even if their implementation was often patchy and uneven (Hudson, 1988). However, the major challenges to 'nothing works' were emerging from American and Canadian research reviews such as Lipsey (1992) and Andrews et al. (1990), and from research in Scotland designed to inform a more effective approach to criminal justice (McIvor, 1990). This material tended, broadly speaking, to favour structured programmes designed to influence attitudes and behaviour, which could be implemented consistently and evaluated. It also offered a realistic prospect of helping some offenders to reduce their offending. A series of publications and 'What Works' conferences gave increasing currency to these ideas (see, for example, McGuire, 1995; Underdown, 1995) and some probation services began to redefine themselves as providers of potentially effective supervision programmes. This new form of commitment to rehabilitation required some considerable changes in thinking: for example, the new research gave little support to unstructured approaches such as relationship-based reactive counselling when applied to persistent offenders, and this had been the characteristic style of many probation officers. When 'nothing worked' the content of supervision might as well be determined by practitioner preference as by anything else, but the re-emergence of effectiveness required a more critical approach to the content of practice and implied some reduction of practitioners' liberty to practice as they please.

If the 1970s in probation were the era of psychosocial treatment and the 1980s the era of 'non-treatment' and diversion from custody, the 1990s may well come to be seen as the era of a new rehabilitationism, still informed by the insights of the non-treatment paradigm (see Raynor and Vanstone, 1994a) but promising a more effective impact on some offenders' behaviour. These two major transformations in probation thinking are not of course the whole story: many practitioners have lived through both without much real change in practice (though there may be changes in the language of their reports and records) and one effect of the 'nothing works' era was to induce in much of the probation service a robust and durable indifference to research. The practical impact of recent developments may also be limited by yet another change in thinking at the political level. In 1993 a new Home Secretary drawn from the right of the Conservative Party decided, presumably for electoral reasons, to depart from the pragmatic non-partisan approach to penal policy which had guided all previous post-war governments and announced in a Party Conference speech that 'prison works' and that the cure for crime was to be found in a more systematically punitive penal policy (Howard, 1993).

This speech signalled a departure from the penal strategy of the 1991 Act and was liberally spiced with expressions of contempt for the views of professionals and academics in the field: from now on, editorials in the Daily Mail and the Sun were to be more important guides to policy. Since then, criminal justice policy has been in a state of some confusion: eye-catching initiatives such as 'boot camps' and electronic tagging coexist with the highest post-war prison population, and the probation service itself has been targeted for unwelcome changes in its training and recruitment in an attempt to change its perceived liberal social work ethos (Dews and Watts, 1994). At the time of writing this chapter the long-term impact of these developments is as unclear as the Conservative Government's electoral prospects, but certainly they represent a third major shift in the official view of probation, if not yet in thinking within the probation service itself. The main aim of this chapter, however, is to trace the interaction between the 'moving target' of changing conceptions of probation and the methods and emphasis of evaluative research, and for this purpose we are more concerned with the earlier changes which have had time to penetrate the consciousness and practice of practitioner and research communities.

Evaluating probation in the 'treatment' era

Reference has already been made to two studies of the late 1950s, Wilkins (1958) and Radzinowicz (1958). These studies were methodologically different, since Radzinowicz documented subsequent offending without comparing it with those subject to other sentences while Wilkins used a comparison group; perhaps not surprisingly, they also came to rather different conclusions about effectiveness, with more negative conclusions in Wilkins' study. However, from the point of view of this chapter it is more interesting to consider where they directed their attention and where they did not. In line with the 'treatment' model, they looked for effects on offenders' subsequent behaviour; they were not interested in criminal justice system issues such as impacts on sentencing, 'market shares' or the tariff level of those supervised. They also have little interest in methods used: probation is regarded as a method in itself, and the package is not unwrapped to see what lies inside. The research agenda was confined to the claims of the treatment model and circumscribed by contemporary assumptions about what probation was for, though Wilkins did at least raise the important question of whether probation's effects were measurably better than those of other disposals.

Soon after this the Home Office launched an ambitious programme of research aimed at classifying probationers and their problems empirically, leading to large and interesting studies such as Davies (1969), and eventually to a focus on what probation officers actually did in response to these problems (Davies, 1974). A significant emerging concern was that probation as psychosocial casework aspired, at least in the textbooks, to a focus on emotional problems (particularly 'underlying' ones) whilst probationers clearly had many social and environmental difficulties which probation officers addressed to varying degrees, often, according to Davies, without much evidence of resulting change. The agenda was still 'treatment' but anxieties were emerging about the fit between the treatment provided and actual needs. The probation service, of course, could claim that caseloads were too high to allow them to show what they could achieve given better resources, and the eventual response to this was a controlled test: the IMPACT study (Intensive Matched Probation and After-Care Treatment) which randomly allocated probationers to normal or 'intensive' caseloads and compared both the work done and the subsequent offending in these two groups - a classic research design for testing 'treatment'.

The results of the study (Folkard et al., 1976) were remarkably little discussed in the probation service but had a significant effect on the research agenda. The probationers in the experimental small caseloads did receive more attention; the nature of the attention was left to the officers, and could mostly be summarised as more of what they would normally do. The overall results were 'small non-significant differences in reconviction in favour of the control cases', and no confirmation that more probation 'treatment' produced better (or any) effects. The one significant exception was that 'the only experimental cases that apparently do much better are those which have been rated as having low criminal tendencies and which perceive themselves as having many problems', a fairly small group and arguably rather untypical of offenders in general, but broadly resembling offenders who showed positive results in other studies (Shaw, 1974; Adams, 1961; Palmer, 1974). One possible interpretation is that the typical content of probation in the 'treatment' era could be helpful to those who were distressed, anxious to change and not particularly criminal. This prefigured later findings about the limited relevance of relationship-based counselling to work with persistent offenders, but the overall conclusion had to be seen as a negative verdict on probation as a general-purpose 'treatment' for crime: most of the 'culprits' were not being 'readjusted', and the Home Office began to turn its research attention elsewhere.

Probation research in the era of diversion

The apparently conclusive demise of 'treatment' produced not only a major shift in policy-makers' views of what probation might realistically achieve but a corresponding shift in focus for the questions asked by evaluative researchers.

The influence of early juvenile justice system studies (e.g. Thorpe et al., 1980) has been mentioned already. These studies paid detailed attention to patterns of decision-making in the juvenile courts in an attempt to measure how the activities of social workers were reducing or increasing incarceration, but showed little interest in the content of supervision or the subsequent behaviour of offenders: the guiding assumption seemed to be that post-custodial reconviction rates for juveniles were already so high that any likely outcome of a community-based project would be an improvement. The Home Office itself had already begun to undertake studies guided by a similar set of assumptions about what it was interesting to measure: as well as early work on police cautions which addressed system issues such as net-widening (Ditchfield, 1976) a substantial programme of evaluative work on the new Community Service Order had been developing in parallel with the final stages of the probation research programme.

Community Service, introduced by the 1972 Criminal Justice Act, was initially implemented on an experimental basis in a number of pilot areas, and the associated Home Office research was primarily concerned with whether it was feasible to implement it; whether courts were using it; and how far it was being used for offenders who would otherwise be sent to prison (Pease et al., 1977; Pease and McWilliams, 1980). In other words, the Community Service research agenda was about effects on systems rather than people, and a complete departure from the 'treatment' agenda: so much so that the decision to extend Community Service to all probation areas was taken before effects on reoffending had been assessed, and issues such as the kinds of help needed or received by offenders and its effects on their behaviour were not addressed until a much later Scottish study (McIvor, 1992). Community Service was intended to influence sentencers rather than offenders, and the research conformed closely to these priorities; other more rehabilitation-oriented innovations such as the Day Training Centres received far less official research attention (Vanstone and Raynor, 1981) and although activities such as social enquiry reports continued to attract interest (Thorpe, 1979), government-sponsored research on the effectiveness of probation virtually ceased after IMPACT. One of the few exceptions to this was a short study of probation day centres (Mair, 1988) which revealingly pointed out that 'it is difficult to assess the success of centres in preventing reoffending; there is little monitoring of the centres in this respect and the main aim of the centres is to provide an alternative to custody'. Otherwise the Home Office Research Studies series during the 1980s was dominated by what has perhaps too dismissively been described as 'administrative criminology' concerned with crime prevention, victim surveys and operational issues in criminal justice agencies.

The dominance of new post-treatment, system-centred aims was underlined by the publication in 1984 of a 'Statement of National Objectives and Priorities' for probation services in England and Wales (Home Office, 1984). This document, the first attempt at a national statement of the probation service's purpose, was clearly informed by the intention to develop community-based supervision in such a way as to reduce custodial sentencing. Social enquiry reports were to be a high priority 'where the court may be prepared to divert an offender from what would otherwise be a custodial sentence' and probation and community service orders were desirable 'especially in cases where custodial sentences would otherwise be imposed'. The Statement was in due course accompanied by the introduction of performance indicators such as the proportion of probationers who were first offenders (intended to fall) and the proportion with previous custodial experience (intended to rise). After-care, presumed to have no diversionary impact, was allocated a lower place in the order of priorities. Nothing was said about the content or methods of supervision.

For the probation service itself matters were not so simple. Community Service seemed to be a success, but the market share of probation orders had been falling through most of the 1970s. Probation orders which could be seen as a credible disposal for more serious offenders would need to offer more demanding and, if possible, effective programmes of supervision. The 1982 Criminal Justice Act encouraged the inclusion of additional requirements in probation orders to facilitate special programmes, but these larger packages needed more content. Juvenile justice specialists were already developing intensive Intermediate Treatment with often quite sophisticated programme content (e.g. Denman, 1982), and probation services began to follow suit with various forms of enhanced probation, despite the reservations of some of their staff (Drakeford, 1983). Occasionally these involved an almost bizarre degree of emphasis on control and discipline (Kent Probation and After-Care Service, 1981) but more often they looked for content which seemed likely to be useful to offenders and was intended to reduce their offending. Among these piecemeal and often unevaluated developments, a few projects took research seriously enough to involve local academics in what became a new style of evaluative study.

Such local projects were typically concerned both with 'market shares' and with impacts on offending, and the combination of modest scale and locally based research allowed for adequate follow-up of both sentencing trends and the behaviour of offenders. Two studies in particular, carried out during the 1980s and published towards the end of the decade (Raynor, 1988; Roberts, 1989) were able to address some of the issues about effectiveness which had almost vanished from the national research agenda, and in both cases some diversion from custody and some impact on reconviction could be reasonably convincingly demonstrated. One of the studies (Raynor, 1988) was also able to document changes in offenders' self-perceived problems and suggested a link between these and subsequent reductions in offending. These attempts to combine the offender-

4   An awareness of social context issues and their effects on the opportunities and priorities of offenders (see, for example, Stewart and Stewart, 1993). Intervention by probation services does not occur in a social vacuum, and we need to find out more about what social problems offenders actually face and what counts for them as improvement. For example, a recent evaluation of through-care work (Maguire et al., 1995) found that much probation activity in this field was directed towards resettlement and reintegration rather than 'confronting offending behaviour', and that this was on the whole valued by those who were being supervised.

5   A more systematic attempt to document and describe the probation inputs that lead to the results. Most studies of the 1970s and 1980s either took the nature of the input for granted or were faced with practice of such diversity that it was difficult to disentangle which inputs were associated with which effects. The emergence of structured programmes and of concern for programme integrity allows a new and possibly more productive approach to the problem of defining inputs.

6   A related point, but possibly a greater professional challenge, is that more information about effectiveness implies more information about ineffectiveness. If some programmes are effective but probation orders with additional requirements are not in aggregate particularly effective, what is this telling us about the quality of some of the unevaluated programmes? A recent study of pre-sentence reports (Gelsthorpe and Raynor, 1995) found that the quality of reports was very variable, but that the better quality reports were more effective. Such findings challenge probation services to go beyond advertising their successes, and to identify and address weaknesses in a systematic way.

Many of these issues of design and methodology argue for a more engaged style of research in which researchers get close to probation activities, to practitioners and to offenders. Paradoxically this is sometimes easier in the under-funded but long-term local study than in national studies which are well resourced but necessarily remote from their subjects and required to produce results within tight time limits. There is a need for more devolution and generalisation in the overall research effort, and for a more systematic use of probation services' own research capacity for evaluation rather than simply to provide management information. Probation practice has usually been more diverse and imaginative than policy, and probation services and their staff last longer than temporary political preoccupations. We need evaluative strategies which will adequately reflect this complexity and help to enhance its effectiveness. Overall, to end on a note of unaccustomed optimism, the prospects for interesting and useful probation research in Britain have never been brighter, and the need for it has never been greater.

References

Adams, S. (1961), 'Interaction between individual interview therapy and treatment amenability in older youth authority wards', in *Inquiries Concerning Kinds of Treatment for Kinds of Offenders*, pp. 27-44, California Board of Corrections, Sacramento,

Andrews, D. A., Zinger, I., Hoge, R. D., Bonta, J., Gendreau, P. and Cullen, F. T. (1990), 'Does correctional treatment work? A clinically relevant and psychologically informed meta-analysis', *Criminology, 28*, 369-904.

Bottoms, A.E. and McWilliams, W. (1979), 'A non-treatment paradigm for probation practice', *British Journal of Social Work, 9*, 159-202.

Brody, S.R. (1976), *The Effectiveness of Sentencing*, Home Office Research Study No. 35, HMSO, London.

Davies, M. (1969), *Probationers in their Social Environment*, Home Office Research Study No. 2, HMSO, London.

Davies, M. (1974), *Social Work in the Environment*, Home Office Research Study No. 21, HMSO, London.

Denman, G. (1982), *Intensive Intermediate Treatment with Juvenile Offenders: a Handbook of Assessment and Groupwork Practice*, Lancaster: Centre of Youth, Crime and Community, Lancaster University.

Dews, V. and Watts, J. (1994), *Review of Probation Officer Recruitment and Qualifying Training*, Home Office, London.

Ditchfield, J. A. (1976), *Police Cautioning in England and Wales*, Home Office Research Study No. 37, HMSO, London.

Drakeford, M. (1983), 'Probation: containment or liberty?', *Probation Journal, 30*, 7-10.

Folkard, M.S., Smith, D.E. and Smith, D.D. (1976), *IMPACT Vol.II*, Home Office Research Study No. 36, HMSO, London.

Foren, R. and Bailey, R. (1968), *Authority in Social Casework* Pergamon,Oxford.

Gelsthorpe, L. and Raynor, P. (1995), 'Quality and effectiveness in probation officers' reports to sentencers', *British Journal of Criminology, 35*, 188-200.

Home Office (1984), *Probation Service in England and Wales: Statement of National Objectives and Priorities*, Home Office, London.

Home Office (1988), *Punishment, Custody and the Community*, Cm 424, HMSO, London.

Home Office (1990a), *Crime, Justice and Protecting the Public*, Cm 965,: HMSO, London.

Home Office (1990b), *Supervision and Punishment in the Community*, Cm 966, HMSO, London.

Hood, R. (1974), *Tolerance and the Tariff*, NACRO, London.

Howard, M,. (Home Secretary) (1993), speech to Conservative Party conference, October.

Hudson, B. (1988), 'Social skills training in practice', *Probation Journal, 35*, 85-91.

Hunt, A. W. (1964), 'Enforcement in probation casework', *British Journal of Delinquency, 4*, 239-252.

Kent Probation and After-Care Service (1981), 'Probation Control Unit: a community-based experiment in intensive supervision' *in Annual Report on the Work of the Medway Centre*, Maidstone: Kent Probation and After-Care Service.

Lipsey, M. (1992), 'Juvenile delinquency treatment: a meta-analytic enquiry into the variability of effects', in T. Cook, H. Cooper, D. S. Cordray, H. Hartmann, L. V. Hedges,R. L. Light, T. A. Louis and F. Mosteller (eds.) *Meta-Analysis for Explanation: a case-book*, pp. 83-127, Russell Sage, New York.

Lipton, D., Martinson, R. and Wilks, J. (1975), *The Effectiveness of Correctional Treatment*, Praeger, New York.

Lloyd, C., Mair, G. and Hough, M. (1994), *Explaining Reconviction Rates: a critical analysis*, Home Office Research Study No. 136, HMSO, London.

Lucas, J., Raynor, P. and Vanstone, M. (1992), *Straight Thinking On Probation one year on*, Mid Glamorgan Probation Service, Bridgend.

Maguire, M., Perroud, B. and Raynor, P. (1995) *Automatic Conditional Release: the first two years*, Report to the Home Office Research and Planning Unit, University of Wales, Cardiff (unpublished).

Mair, G. (1988), *Probation Day Centres*, Home Office Research Study No. 150, HMSO, London.

Mair, G., Lloyd, C., Nee, C. and Sibbitt, R. (1994), *Intensive Probation in England and Wales: an evaluation*, Home Office Research Study No. 133, HMSO, London.

Martinson, J. (1974), 'What works? Questions and answers about prison reform', *The Public Interest, 35*, 22-54.

McGuire, J. ed. (1995), *What Works: Reducing Offending*, Wiley, Chichester.

McGuire, J. and Priestley, P. (1985), *Offending Behaviour*, Batsford, London.

McIvor, G. (1990), *Sanctions for Serious or Persistent Offenders*, Social Work Research Centre, Stirling.

McIvor, G. (1992), *Sentenced to Serve*, Avebury, Aldershot.

McWilliams, W. (1989), 'An expressive model for evaluating probation practice', *Probation* Journal, *36*, 58-64.

Monger, M. (1964), *Casework in Probation*, Butterworth, London.

Palmer, T. (1974), 'The Youth Authority's Community Treatment Project', *Federal Probation, 38*, 3-14.

Pease, K., Billingham S. and Earnshaw, I. (1977), *Community Service Assessed in 1976*, Home Office Research Study No. 39, HMSO, London.

Pease, K. and McWilliams, W. eds. (1980), *Community Service by Order*, Scottish Academic Press, Edinburgh.

Petersilia, J. (1990), 'Conditions that permit intensive supervision programmes to survive', *Crime and Delinquency, 36*, 126-45.

Radzinowicz, L. (1958), *The Results of Probation*, Macmillan, London.

Raynor, P. (1988), *Probation as an Alternative to Custody*, Avebury, Aldershot.

Raynor, P. and Vanstone, M. (1994a), 'Probation practice, effectiveness and the non-treatment paradigm', *British Journal of Social Work, 24*, 387-404.

Raynor, P., and Vanstone, M. (1994b), *Straight Thinking On Probation: third interim evaluation report: reconvictions within 12 months*, Mid Glamorgan Probation Service. Bridgend.

Roberts, C.H. (1989), *Hereford and Worcester Probation Service Young Offender Project: first evaluation report*, Department of Social and Administrative Studies, Oxford.

Ross, R.R., Fabiano, E.A. and Ewles, C.D. (1988), 'Reasoning and Rehabilitation', *International Journal of Offender Therapy and Comparative Criminology, 32*, 29-35.

Shaw, M. (1974), *Social Work in Prison*, Home Office Research Study No. 22, HMSO, London.

Smith, G. and Cantley, C. (1984), 'Pluralistic evaluation', in J. Lishman (ed.), *Evaluation*, pp. 140-162, University of Aberdeen, Aberdeen.

Stewart, G. and Stewart, J. (1993), *Social Circumstances of Younger Offenders Under Supervision*, Association of Chief Officers of Probation, London..

Thorpe, D.H., Smith, D., Green, C.J. and Paley, J. (1980), *Out of Care*, Allen & Unwin, London.

Thorpe, J. (1979), *Social Inquiry Reports: a survey*, Home Office Research Study No. 48, HMSO, London.

Underdown, A. (1995), *Effectiveness of Community Supervision: performance and potential*, Greater Manchester Probation Service, Manchester.

Vanstone, M. (1993), 'A 'missed opportunity' reassessed: the influence of the Day Training Centre experiment on the criminal justice system and probation practice', *British Journal of Social Work, 23*, 213-29.

Vanstone, M. and Raynor, P. (1981) 'Diversion from prison: a partial success and a missed opportunity', *Probation Journal, 28*, 85-89.

Von Hirsch, A. (1976), *Doing Justice*, Hill and Wang, New York.

Wilkins, L. T. (1958), 'A small comparative study of the results of probation', *British Journal of Delinquency, 8*, 201-9.

3 The limitations of reconviction rates

George Mair, Charles Lloyd and Mike Hough

The effectiveness of penal measures has almost always focused on recidivism and, in the UK at least, this has meant reconviction rates. The analysis of reconviction rates has had a central place in post-war criminology, but for too often they have been treated with more respect and reverence than they deserve. Too rarely has it been recognised that reconviction rates are artefacts constructed from what is all too often rather dubious data. With the renewed emphasis on evaluating the effectiveness of sentences which has occurred in the last few years, and a confidence that the 'Nothing Works' myth has at last been destroyed for good (see McGuire, 1995), it is imperative that we understand as far as possible the limitations of reconviction rates and recognise how far they can help.

Although reconviction rates are used so often to assess the effectiveness of court sentences, there has been little discussion of the advantages and drawbacks of using them in this way. Reconviction rates tend to be approached as a neutral, technical matter; it is taken for granted that they are unproblematic and easily understood - yet this could not be further from the truth. There have been occasional comments on the inadequacies of reconviction rates in some well-known British studies (e.g. Hood and Sparks, 1970; Brody, 1976), and there is one American book which focuses entirely upon the concept of recidivism (Maltz, 1984); but researchers tend to carry on using a measure which they are aware is flawed, but only very rarely make any attempt to draw attention to the flaws and what these might mean for their analyses.

This chapter discusses the various methodological and practical factors which limit the direct usefulness of reconviction rates and render problematic their utilisation as a simple measure of the success of sentences. While a cursory glance at what follows might lead to the conclusion that reconviction rates are not especially helpful and should be consigned to the criminological dustbin, this would be a mistake; reconviction rates are one of the essential tools of the trade of the criminologist. The aim here is to try to clarify as far as possible some of the key issues around reconviction rates in order that they may be used more appropriately and with a fuller understanding of what they mean. This is important as it is all too easy to condemn one disposal for a reconviction rate of 70 per cent and praise another for a rate of 35 per cent, particularly if (as is usually the case) nothing is known about the operation and organisation of the disposals in question and what they aimed to do. With continuous pressure on organisations to demonstrate effectiveness, crude measures leading to simplistic judgements must be avoided.

Problems associated with reconviction rates

1. The aims of sentencing

Court disposals aim to do a variety of things in addition to discouraging further offending. Retribution, reparation, general deterrence and denunciation are all included in the objectives of sentencing but cannot be measured by the use of reconviction rates. Michael Maltz (1984) has listed a series of correctional goals which he groups into three categories: goals related to the offender, goals related to society and goals related to the correctional institution. He argues that reconviction rates should not be used in measuring the goals of the second or third categories, and cannot be used to measure all of the goals of the first group:

> With such diverse correctional goals one cannot expect a single measure of effectiveness to cover the waterfront; measures of similar diversity are required.

By a single-minded concentration on reconviction rates, the other aims of sentencing are forgotten or relegated to a minor role. This may be acceptable if there is general agreement that the primary aim of sentencing is the reduction of reoffending and that nothing else counts for very much, but it would be dangerous to assume that such agreement exists (the controversy aroused by the Criminal Justice Act 1991 which led to it being watered-down within months of its implementation should serve as an adequate reminder of the lack of agreement). The symbolic nature of the trial and sentencing may be at least as important as its more practical objectives, but that cannot be measured by studying reconviction rates.

35

2. What is meant by reconviction ?

It may seem unduly pedantic to ask what precisely is meant by reconviction, but this is an important question, the answer to which has serious implications for the way in which reconviction data are collected, analysed and interpreted. In the USA, recidivism (which is what is being measured by reconviction rates) has been defined in a variety of ways. Maltz (1984) lists nine categories which have been used along with some of their qualifying conditions

Arrest: number of arrests; recorded police contact; court appearance, time elapsed before the first re-arrest; did conviction result ?

Reconviction: jail or prison sentence; seriousness of offence; sentence.

Incarceration: type of facility; seriousness of offence.

Parole violation: nature of the violation; seriousness of the infraction; was it police-initiated?

Parole suspension: new offence; number of suspensions.

Parole revocation: new offence; seriousness of the offence; average number of good days on parole.

Offence: seriousness; number; new offence.

Absconding: was an absconder warrant issued?

Probation: proportion re-detained; length of time detained; number of violations; violation warrant.

Matters are further complicated by the fact that in some studies more than one definition has been used; and where the same general definition has been used by two studies, different specific definitions may have been applied. All of this makes for considerable confusion.

In the UK such a wide range of definitions has not been apparent, but this does not mean that reconvictions have a hard-edged clarity. In the first place, the term reconviction does not usually apply to the number of convictions in a court for separate offences at a single appearance. If this were the case, offenders would commonly be found with many reconvictions within a relatively short time as many minor offences are often dealt with on only one or two court appearances. Reconviction is generally used to mean an appearance in court where there has been at least one finding of guilt, irrespective of how many offences were dealt with on a single appearance (and this is how it will be used here). It is perhaps worth noting that the recent reconviction study by Lloyd et al. (1994) showed that both the actual number of convictions and the number of appearances had an effect on reconviction rates: 'there is a pronounced tendency for reconviction rates to increase as the average number of convictions per appearance increases'. In future, it may be worth looking in further detail at the impact of the number of convictions as well as the number of previous guilty appearances.

In addition, it should be noted that guilty findings for all kinds of offences are not normally counted in calculating reconviction rates; the usual approach is to count only Standard List offences, which ignores many minor offences and therefore provides an underestimate of the number of reconvictions. To count all offences, including the most minor, may seem to be excessive and unduly pedantic but if reconviction studies are to move forward towards more sophisticated models and take account of the seriousness of offending, it may be necessary to become more inclusive.

3. *Reconviction is not reoffending*

Reconvictions are only a proxy measure for reoffending, and this needs to be borne in mind when using and interpreting reconviction studies. By no means all those offenders who, after conviction, go on to commit further offences are caught, and not all those who are caught are convicted in court. Latest estimates from the British Crime Survey (BCS) suggest that for every 100 offences committed only two result in a criminal conviction. While reporting a crime to the police may be a necessary step towards the conviction of an offender in court, it is by no means a sufficient one: only 50 per cent of offences are reported to the police, only 30 per cent are recorded by the police as a crime; seven per cent of crimes are cleared up, and three per cent result in a caution or conviction. The gap widens at every stage in the process (see Home Office, 1993, p.29).

Indeed, the gap is not uniform for all types of crime, and some idea of the problems can be seen from the results of the BCS. In comparing information from the BCS to notifiable offences recorded by the police, it was found that while 92 per cent of burglaries with loss and 99 per cent of motor vehicle theft were reported, only 40 per cent of robberies and 27 per cent of vandalism were reported to the police (Mayhew and Aye Maung, 1992). Self-report surveys may go some way towards narrowing the gap (though these have their own considerable problems), but it is impossible to close it completely. Thus the use of reconviction rates means that under-estimation is always present, but we cannot be sure of its extent and this is particularly problematic for any measure of effectiveness.

4.   *Is there a 'correct' follow-up period'?*

How long should the follow-up period for a reconviction study be ? This is a key question and the answer will have a significant effect upon reconviction rates.   Clearly, a two year reconviction study will provide fewer reconvictions than a five year study, but how much extra value is offered by the latter if the average reconviction rate in a two year study is 65 per cent and that in a five year study is 75 per cent ? A five year study will necessarily take much longer to carry out and by the time such a study is completed, the original interest in the results may have petered out.   Indeed, if one wishes to use reconviction rates to find out why a sentence seems to be a success or a failure, then it is probably not worth waiting for more than five years before being able to identify 'good' or 'bad' programmes and then trying to isolate what made them succeed or fail.   The political agenda does not run to such a leisurely timetable.

A six-month study may be all that is necessary, even if a further 30 per cent of reconvictions take place during the subsequent 18 months; the decision lies in what is known about trends and patterns of offending.   For example, research has suggested that prisoners have a relatively delayed pattern of reconviction, which raises the question of whether a longer follow-up period than two years is required (Lloyd et al., 1994; Phillpotts and Lancucki, 1979).   For sex offenders a follow-up period of at least five years is considered desirable due to their patterns of offending; the proportion reconvicted grows slowly but consistently over time.   For burglars, six months or a year may be adequate.   The usual period is two years, but studies of longer and shorter periods would be helpful as would the application of survival analysis techniques.

5.   *When do you start counting ?*

Closely linked to the question of the length of follow-up period, is the question of when one starts counting reconvictions.   Again, it is reasonably obvious that if one was to begin at the start of all sentences, then those in custody would tend to have lower reconviction rates simply because they would not be able to reoffend (except within prison) for the full follow-up period.   The answer for those in custody is to begin counting from the date of release.   For community penalties, however, counting conventionally begins on the date of sentence.   It might be more appropriate - but more complex - to begin from the date when the community penalty actually begins; but in any event, this is normally within a few days of sentence.

Parole, or automatic conditional release, raises several issues. Should counting begin from the date of release from custody, or at the end of the period of supervision by the probation service: if the former, does reconviction during the supervision period constitute a failure of prison or of supervision; if the latter, then the risk of reconviction will be considerably reduced if the period under supervision is completed successfully.

There is a case of sorts for counting reconvictions from the end of a community penalty on the argument that the effectiveness of 'treatment' should be assessed only when it has been completed (and, in the case of prison, counting starts on the date of release). On the other hand, however, it could be argued that the probation service tries to hold offenders from further offending while they are subject to supervision, but cannot be held responsible for their behaviour post-supervision. In any case, those who successfully complete their orders are, by definition, better bets than those who are breached.

6. The time lag between offending and conviction

Related to the two previous issues are problems arising from the practice of using date of conviction (or reconviction) as a proxy for date of offending. Some offenders offend prior to their 'target' appearance, but are reconvicted after they have begun their sentence - these are false positives and have been termed pseudo-reconvictions by Lloyd et al. (1994). Conversely, towards the end of the follow-up period, some offenders will offend but not be reconvicted until after the follow-up period has been completed (false negatives). In the first case, reconviction rates will be inflated, while in the second they will be under-estimated. Reconviction studies have usually ignored the problem of false positives and false negatives, but the distorting effects of pseudo-reconvictions in particular could be substantial. It would seem especially relevant to investigate the possibility that there are differences between sentences in the extent of pseudo-reconvictions. It would seem plausible, for example, that those who have completed prison sentences will be less likely than those starting probation or community service to be convicted of offences pre-dating their sentence, simply because of the greater lapse of time. Offences will come to court while the offender is still in prison, or else the Crown Prosecution Service may decide not to proceed.

A recent reconviction study carried out by the Home Office Research and Planing Unit (Lloyd et al., 1994) investigated the effect of pseudo-reconvictions and found, as expected, that community disposals were associated with fewer pseudo-reconvictions than prison sentences.

Table 3.1 shows the impact of removing pseudo-reconvictions from four sentence groups.

Table 3.1
Predicted and actual reconviction rates 1987, correcting for pseudo-reconvictions

Sentence group	Raw % reconvicted	Adjusted % reconvicted	Predicted % reconvicted	Total No.
Prison	56	54	53	9,615
Probation	49	43	45	2,448
Community service orders	56	49	52	2,394
4A/4B	68	63	60	3,354

Source: Lloyd et al., 1994, Table 5.4

In the case of straight probation, community service orders and probation orders with 4A/4B requirements, the reconviction rates fell by six, seven and five percentage points respectively by removing the pseudo-reconvictions (subtracting the figures in the 'adjusted' column from those in the 'raw' column). For prison, the fall was only two per cent. And the effect of doing this is considerable: simply comparing the raw rate with the predicted rate, it looks as if both straight probation and community service orders were associated with a reconviction rate four per cent higher than that predicted. By taking pseudo-reconvictions into account, probation's reconviction rate becomes two per cent lower than predicted, while that for community service becomes three per cent lower.

Unfortunately, a similar analysis for false negatives has not been carried out, but there are two considerations which argue against there being a significant problem here. In the first place, there is no reason to suspect a difference between the sentence groups analogous to that predicted and substantiated for pseudo-reconvictions. Second, in looking simply at whether offenders are reconvicted or not within two years, only those false positives or false negatives that occur in the absence of any other reconvictions are relevant. It is unlikely that large numbers of offenders will keep a clean sheet for almost two years but then reoffend and be reconvicted shortly after the two years has elapsed.

A further factor which could play a part in pseudo-reconvictions is whether the offender is bailed or remanded in custody prior to his/her target sentence. If the former, then the offender could have carried out further offending which might well have been dealt with after the target sentence has commenced; a remand in custody, however, would preclude further offending until sentence has been passed. Although recent research has shown that offending while on bail is not as common as is often claimed (Morgan, 1992), reconviction rates will be affected by the bail/remand decision - with a differential impact on custodial and community penalties.

7. *Equating reconviction with failure*

Reconviction rates have, on the whole, been used as a crude, dichotomous measure whereby reconviction equals failure while non-reconviction equals success. This implies that all reconvictions are of equal severity (although, as noted earlier, certain types of offences are not included in reconviction analyses). Thus, an offender who was convicted of a shop theft of low value and reconvicted of a major domestic burglary would be counted as no more of a failure than one who had been sentenced for street robbery and reconvicted for a minor shop theft (not, perhaps it should be added, by sentencers who would be likely to reflect the difference in offences in terms of sentence). In the same way, an offender who, post-conviction, continued to offend every three or four months as he/she had done prior to sentence, would be judged no more of a failure than one whose rate of offending dropped from every two months to every nine months.

Differences in the kind of offences involved in reconviction and in the rate of reconviction should ideally be part of any reconviction study.

8. *Comparing reconviction rates for different sentences*

A common approach to reconviction rates is to compare different sentences (or different examples of the same sentence). Offenders are not sentenced to different disposals randomly, however, and to compare the reconviction rates of disposals without taking some account of this would be misleading. But trying to match offenders with different sentences is difficult simply because offenders with different characteristics receive different sentences. In any event, collecting fully adequate data for matching purposes is, logistically, almost impossible; criminal history is relatively easy to collate (although the reliability of the data should be borne in mind), but how much - if any - social information is necessary and how can one be certain that all key variables have been matched ?

Random allocation is one way around this difficulty, but this is not without its own problems. The random allocation of offenders to different sentences can easily offend principles of equity and would be seen (with some justification) by the judiciary as interference with their decisions. There is no doubt that ethical issues can arise if offenders found guilty of less serious crimes receive more serious sentences for the sake of research, and there are clear public safety issues to be considered if those found guilty of serious offences are given community penalties for the same reason. Random allocation to different programmes under the same sentence is a more feasible option, and it would be worth exploring this more often. It should be added, however, that it is difficult to ensure that allocation is carried out randomly in practice, and this is a problem which has bedevilled many experiments.

One way of getting around this problem has been displayed in Table 3.1. A predicted reconviction rate is calculated for each disposal and this is compared to the actual reconviction rate. If the actual rate is lower than that predicted, then one can assume that the sentence in question is having a positive effect on reconvictions; while if the actual rate is higher than that predicted, the sentence is having a negative effect. This is a better approach than trying to compare different sentences by matching offenders, although there remain difficulties: it may not be the sentence which is having the positive or negative effect but some characteristic of the offenders; and even if it is the sentence, unless a thorough process evaluation has been carried out it will be impossible to say how the sentence is having its effect.

9. The effect of policing and prosecution practice

Other factors, which are difficult to quantify, can have an impact upon reconviction rates. Police action is one obvious element: we know that police forces have different clear-up rates - and these will result in different reconviction rates. Different police patrolling practices and targeting will mean that certain offenders will have a greater chance of being arrested and reconvicted than others; for example, those with long records may be subject to greater surveillance, and where offenders live may be a significant factor in their likelihood of being reconvicted (cf. Gottfredson and Taylor, 1986). Over time, the national clear-up rate has been falling, and this will inevitably make the interpretation of reconviction trends difficult.

Police cautioning practices will also have an effect on reconviction rates. While cautions are not convictions and could not be counted as such, any increase in cautioning over a given period is likely to lead to offences that previously would have resulted in a conviction ending in a caution. Thus, any significant increase in cautioning is likely to depress reconviction rates. At present, neither informal nor formal cautions are centrally recorded, making it difficult to gauge the extent or influence of changes in cautioning practice.

The discontinuance of cases by the Crown Prosecution Service will have a similar effect. Cases can be discontinued both when evidence is weak and when, despite firm evidence, a prosecution is considered not to be in the public interest (the defendant might be old, for example, or unwell). Again, as discontinuances increase, reconviction rates will fall. There have been marked shifts in both cautioning and prosecution practice over time (especially over the last decade) complicating the analysis of trends in reconvictions. And, of course, there are also marked differences by area.

10. *An adequate and accessible data-base*

Reconviction studies need access to criminal records and this has by no means been easy to arrange in the past. Two national data-bases are available: that held at the National Identification Service (NIS, the old Criminal Records Office) and the Offenders Index (OI) held by the Home Office Research and Statistics Directorate. In the past, Offenders Index data were held on microfiche which presented resource problems for the extraction of information. Since computerisation in 1991, however, the OI now yields samples more quickly and more fully than before (Keith, 1993). With regard to NIS data, these are not yet computerised, which has meant that large-scale reconviction studies could only be carried out with considerable clerical effort. Computerisation is now underway at NIS and this will make matters much easier.

In very large data-bases there are likely to be problems with missing data, miscoded cases, etc. In a search for criminal records it is quite likely that as many as 30 per cent of names will not be found for one reason or another. For example, in the reconviction study carried out by Lloyd et al., (1994) the *offender* was not found on the OI in three per cent of the prison cases, nine per cent of community service cases, seven per cent of 4A/4B cases, and ten per cent of straight probation cases. Similarly, in the same study, a matching OI *court appearance* was not found in 15 per cent of prison cases, 22 per cent of CS cases, 22 per cent of 4A/4B cases, and 19 per cent of straight probation cases. If such cases are randomly distributed then this should not be a problem, but there is no way of knowing at present whether such cases are random. A comparative study of the NIS and OI data-bases is long overdue and this could help to clarify the extent of bias in each.

Finally, there is the thorny problem of how reconviction rates are interpreted. There is an unfortunate tendency to conclude simplistically that a high reconviction rate means failure and therefore the sentence or programme has failed. In the first place, however, all too often this judgement is made in the absence of any hard information about the operation and organisation of the programme.   The failure may have been due to lack of resources, poor implementation, untrained staff, a weak theoretical basis or a combination of these; the actual content of the programme may not have been at fault.   The end result may be the premature termination of a programme which has not had a chance to be fully evaluated.   Similarly, if a low reconviction rate is found, a programme may be judged too soon as a success (it may be a result of initial enthusiasm, for example, or the targeting of low-risk offenders); rapid expansion may follow without any real basis and in the longer term disillusionment will result after further evaluation.   If a sentence is successfully targeting offenders at high risk of reconviction (17-20 year old males convicted of burglary, with six or more previous convictions and previous experience of custody), then it is almost inevitable that the reconviction rate for the sentence will be high.

Second, if an unacceptably high overall reconviction rate is found to be associated with a certain sentence, it would surely be a mistake to condemn all specific examples of that sentence.   A recent study of probation centres found that the overall reconviction rate was 63 per cent, but that several centres had rates of 75 per cent or more, while others fell below 45 per cent (Mair and Nee, 1992).   Such differences amongst various examples of the same sentence raise important questions which are hidden by looking at reconviction rates solely at a national level.   Although they raise problems of their own, local reconviction studies need to be carried out.

Nationally-based reconviction rates are probably more useful as indicators of performance than as measures of effectiveness.   Carter and his colleagues have recently categorised performance indicators into three types: dials, tin-openers, and alarm bells.   Although there are obvious overlaps between the three types, reconviction rates seem - at present - most suited to be tin-openers.   As such, they will lead to more detailed questions and investigation:

> They do not give answers but prompt interrogation and inquiry,
> and by themselves provide an incomplete and inaccurate picture.
> (Carter et al., 1992)

Using reconviction rates

None of the problems associated with reconviction rates should lead to the conclusion that they should be banished from the criminologist's lexicon. On the contrary, the aim of detailing their limitations is to urge a more cautious, sceptical and more sophisticated approach to the use of reconviction rates. Reconviction rates can serve as key indicators of performance for both community and custodial penalties; but they should be included in formal lists of key performance indicators only if they are interpreted with care and with a full understanding of their limitations.

While comparing the effectiveness of different sentences may be fraught with difficulties and caveats, such an exercise is a necessity. One of the reasons for the importance of reconviction rates as a performance indicator is that they can be used for various sentences, unlike other possible measures (such as diversion from custody or incapacitation). Nor should it be forgotten that there are considerable problems with measuring any social phenomena, as Maltz (1984) reminds us:

> The measurement of poverty, educational attainment, intelligence, self-esteem, socioeconomic status, social structure or peer-group relationships is no less difficult than the measurement of recidivism.

It is time to consider other possible measure of the effectiveness of sentences (Mair, 1991), and certainly other performance indicators will be necessary, but these should be developed in addition to reconviction rates and not as an alternative to them. Reconviction rates cannot and should not be ignored - but neither should they be accepted uncritically.

Note

This chapter is a slightly redrafted version of Chapter 3 of *Explaining Reconviction Rates: a critical analysis* by Charles Lloyd, George Mair and Mike Hough (London: HMSO, 1994).

References

Brody, S. (1976), *The Effectiveness of Sentencing: a review of the literature*, Home Office Research Study No.35, HMSO, London.

Carter, N., Klein, R. and Day. P. (1992), *How Organisations Measure Success: the use of performance indicators in government*, Routledge, London.

Gottfredson, S.D. and Taylor, R.B. (1986), 'Person-environment interactions in the prediction of recidivism'. In J. M. Byrne, and R. J. Sampson, (eds.) *The Social Ecology of Crime*, Springer-Verlag, New York.

Hood, R. and Sparks, R. (1970), *Key Issues in Criminology*, Weidenfeld and Nicolson, London.

Keith, S. (1993), *The Offender's Tale: Janus studies*, HMSO, London.

Lloyd, C., Mair, G. and Hough, M. (1994), *Explaining Reconviction Rates: a critical analysis*, Home Office Research Study No.136, HMSO, London.

Mair, G. (1991), 'What works - nothing or everything ? Measuring the effectiveness of sentences', *Home Office Research Bulletin*, *30*, 3-8.

Mair, G. and Nee, C. (1992), 'Day centre reconviction rates', *British Journal of Criminology*, *32*, 329-339.

Maltz, M. (1984), *Recidivism*, Academic Press, London.

Mayhew, P. and Aye Maung, N. (1992), *Surveying Crime: findings from the 1992 British Crime Survey*, Research Findings No.2, Home Office Research and Statistics Department, London.

McGuire, J. (ed) (1995), *What Works: reducing reoffending - guidelines from research and practice*, John Wiley and Sons, Chichester.

Morgan, P. (1992), *Offending While on Bail: a survey of recent studies*, Research and Planning Unit Paper No.65, Home Office, London.

Phillpotts, G. and Lancucki, L. (1979), *Previous Convictions, Sentence and Reconviction: a statistical study of a sample of 5,000 offenders convicted in January 1971*, Home Office Research Study No.53, HMSO, London.

4 Evaluating the 'tackling offending' initiative: effects without a cause

Adrian James and Keith Bottomley

> It is regrettable that over the years so little attention has been paid by criminology to the development of policy and the impact that this has on criminal justice practice ... All too often it seems to be assumed that policy initiatives are carefully and rationally prepared on the basis of in-depth knowledge about practice, and that these are unproblematically communicated to practitioners who then simply put them into practice. For a variety of reasons, this simple, rational model is rarely achieved in the real world. (Mair et al., 1994, p. 120)

Context

This chapter differs from most of the others in this collection because rather than consider the evaluation of a specific form of intervention with offenders, it addresses the issues raised by the evaluation of a government initiative which was intended to address a much broader agenda. Part of this was to address the problems presented to the criminal justice system and the community by a particularly difficult, demanding and numerous category of offenders - young adult offenders. Dealing with these had become an issue because the 1980s had witnessed growing public and political concern about the use of custody, the steadily rising prison population and the contribution of young adult offenders to this, and the consequent problems of prison overcrowding and management.

At another level entirely, however, this initiative was a key part of the government's strategy to effect a shift in the orientation of the probation service in order to encourage it to embrace an approach to dealing with offenders in the community which was consistent with its developing broad-based strategy for the reorientation of the criminal justice system. These concerns were clearly reflected in criminal justice policies developed during the 1980s and in the changing role of the probation service within these (see Mair, 1989).

The overall aim of this strategy was to move progressively to a desert-based model of criminal justice which would be compatible with the generally libertarian ideology which was the hallmark of so many other areas of the Government's social and economic policies. Within this aim, there were a number of inter-related objectives, foremost amongst which were: increasing the use of community-based sentences for non-dangerous offenders; reducing the cost of offending to the taxpayer by reserving the expensive option of imprisonment for those from whom the public needed protection; moving the probation service centre stage in the provision of community-based penalties within the criminal justice system; ensuring that such penalties were seen as tough, politically credible and therefore viable as part of a policy aimed at reducing the use made of imprisonment; achieving more political control over both the ethos and the standards of the probation service, thereby making it less autonomous, more accountable, and therefore more responsive to government policies; encouraging the development of partnerships in the delivery of services throughout the criminal justice system; and achieving better value for money in the criminal justice system and in the probation service by targeting resources.

The first occasion when these different elements were pulled together and explicitly articulated as a coherent part of this strategy was in the Green Paper, *Punishment, Custody and the Community* (Home Office, 1988a), in which the Government expressed particular concern about the increasing use of custody for young adult offenders (aged 17 to 20) and sought to build on successes in the management of juvenile offending by developing similar local inter-agency initiatives. Noting that 'The policies for juvenile offenders will not be entirely suitable for the older age group, but some features can be the same' (Home Office, 1988a, para. 2.18), the Government sought to encourage co-ordinated local policies aimed at diverting young adult offenders from crime and custody, and to build upon initiatives already taken by some probation areas and voluntary organizations which did not require new legislation. Shortly after the Green Paper was published, the Home Office set out its short-term strategy for targeting this age group in a circular letter to Chief Probation Officers under the title of *Tackling Offending: An Action Plan* (17 August 1988).

This proposed a two-pronged approach whereby firstly, local action plans should be drawn up by each probation area, in consultation with the courts, police and other relevant agencies, to provide initiatives under existing statutory powers which were aimed specifically at the diversion of young adult offenders; and secondly, intensive probation programmes should be set up by probation services in selected areas, 'exclusively for offenders who would otherwise receive custodial sentences' (Home Office, 1988b, p. 3). The second element of this approach was evaluated by the Home Office Research and Planning Unit (see Mair et al., 1994), but the evaluation of the first element was contracted out to the Centre for Criminology and Criminal Justice at the University of Hull. The results of this research have been fully reported elsewhere, as have the background to the initiative and some of the research issues involved (Bottomley et al., 1992 and 1993; James and Bottomley, 1994). The purpose of this chapter, however, is to consider the methodological issues involved in such an evaluation in more detail.

Methodological issues

As Mair has helpfully observed, there is an important distinction to be drawn between *process* evaluation and *outcome* evaluation:

> Process evaluation concentrates upon assessing how a project was put into practice, what actually happens on the ground, and relating this to the intended impact of the project. Outcome evaluation, on the other hand, is concerned with the impact of the project - how far does it achieve what it was planned to achieve. The point to emphasise is that both are necessary for a full evaluation. (Mair, 1994, p. 10)

The 'Tackling Offending' initiative, however, raised some important and difficult questions in terms of its evaluation, not only because of the need to address both process and outcome issues but also because of the problem of defining these in relation to such a broad-based initiative as this, the need to explore the complex relationship between these two dimensions, and the difficulties of developing an appropriate research strategy and methodology.

The evaluation primarily revolved around three elements: the way in which local action plans, required under the 'Tackling Offending' initiative, had been formulated and developed; the way in which these action plans had been implemented; and the effects of action plans on the use of custody for young adult offenders. The study involved a detailed investigation of these issues in two broadly comparable probation areas, but in order to put these case studies into the broader national context, it also involved an analysis of all of the action plans submitted to the Home Office by probation areas.

In addition, a postal survey of all Chief Probation Officers was undertaken in order to gather information about how each area had responded to the 'Tackling Offending' initiative. This included a range of details reflecting the requirements of the 'Tackling Offending' initiative: the consultation processes used in formulating action plans; initiatives taken as a result of the 'Tackling Offending' initiative; the time scales for any such developments; any special provisions for female and ethnic minority offenders; the contribution of sentencers to the process; the effects of the local action plan; and information concerning the monitoring of the use of custody. These issues presented a number of problems in terms of evaluation.

Methodological constraints

In one sense, the objectives of the study were clear, since the aims and objectives of the initiative being evaluated were articulated in the circular letter which promulgated the 'Tackling Offending' initiative. In another sense, however, this clarity was deceptive and the study raised a number of methodological problems. Therefore, before presenting some of the main findings of the evaluation and addressing important issues of the relationship between empirical methods and conclusions that emerged from this study, brief mention must be made of a number of methodological constraints that influenced this evaluation. It was apparent that the majority of the issues on which the study was required to focus concerned the processes of formulation and implementation, and that the only major explicit focus on the outcome of the initiative concerned its impact on the use of custody for young adult offenders. As a result, it seemed likely from the outset that there might be problems in relating our findings on the processes to the evidence on the outcome or impact of the initiative.

An additional problem stemmed from the fact that the study did not commence until March 1990, some time after the initiative had been launched. Consequently, as far as the formulation and consultation processes were concerned, the study was necessarily retrospective. We were therefore unable to observe directly any of the key processes and had to draw on secondary and *post hoc* accounts of these processes. As a result, the study had to deal with temporal problems, as well as the difficulty of assessing qualitatively different research phenomena - processes and outcomes.

Related to and stemming from this are important epistemological questions. Process data are different from outcome data since although both are descriptive, they describe different facets of the complex realities which must be evaluated, and describe them in different ways. Outcome data, which are so often the preferred form of data for evaluative studies in the criminal justice system (typically although not necessarily, in the form of rates of offending, reconviction, imprisonment, or other activities), are often presented as being 'hard' when, as it has been clearly demonstrated so many times, the utility of such data in terms of evaluating the 'success' of projects can be quite limited. In contrast, process data, which can often do so much to increase our knowledge and understanding of the factors which influence the way in which particular projects or initiatives are implemented and which so often illustrate the difficulties inherent in making clear and simple judgements about effectiveness, are often seen as intrinsically 'soft' and therefore less 'reliable', or valuable.

Such issues assumed particular importance when assessing the action plans which were a central component of the 'Tackling Offending' initiative, since these themselves were the *output* of the process by which they were formulated and as such, it became clear that they were multi-purpose documents which reflected a number of different agendas. This raised a number of issues in terms of evaluating a policy initiative such as this, a key problem being that of interpreting the action plans sent by Chief Probation Officers to the Home Office and of understanding not only what the plans said, but also what they actually meant in practice.

Thus, for example, at a methodological level, in evaluating the impact of the 'Tackling Offending' initiative in terms of the development of measures to reduce the use of custody for young adult offenders in probation areas, what weight should be given to statements of intent, of which there were many examples in the action plans submitted? And at an epistemological level, how much weight and what meaning can be attached to carefully drafted constructions describing consultation processes, developments and intentions, which are submitted by the chief officers of agencies noted for their tradition of autonomy (which was, in part, the reason for the 'Tackling Offending' initiative), which clearly may therefore have considerable strategic importance in preserving that organizational autonomy by presenting images of compliance?

Objectives and empirical measures

In an effort to overcome part of this particular set of problems, the analysis of the action plans drew a distinction between those services which had made some provision - i.e. had taken action - and those which intended to do so. Although this was a helpful distinction to make at the level of increasing our understanding of what had *not* yet happened, it could not help in terms of assessing certain elements of areas' responses to the 'Tackling Offending' initiative because neither we nor the Home Office had the means of determining the extent to which such intentions would be put into practice. Thus, action plans which were high in terms of intentions but low in terms of action could present the picture of a very positive response to the 'Tackling Offending' initiative, making evaluation of its impact difficult in terms of the action plans alone.

To supplement these data therefore, a postal survey of probation areas was undertaken seeking information about the issues outlined above. This achieved a very high response rate - 91 per cent - and we were not therefore faced with the problem of how much weight to attach to data gathered from questionnaires to which the response rate had been poor. This yielded some useful information about both process and outcome. In terms of process, the responses gave a reasonably clear picture about initiatives which had been taken, about the time scales for the implementation of local action plans, and gave sometimes very detailed accounts of the consultations into which services had entered, both within and outwith their own organizations. It also became clear that a number of services had included initiatives aimed at diverting young adult offenders from custody in their action plans which had already either been planned or were in effect before the 'Tackling Offending' initiative. This particular aspect of the study was therefore made more problematic because it was not always clear whether initiatives were a response to the 'Tackling Offending' initiative or not.

The questionnaires also provided information about outcomes in terms of the perceived impact of the 'Tackling Offending' initiative on the use of custody for young adult offenders. In addition to the data generated by the specific requests for information, however, the questionnaires also gave Chief Officers the opportunity to express their views of the initiative, giving some valuable personal insights into the way in which the 'Tackling Offending' initiative had been launched and managed by the Home Office.

The epistemological question then arises of how to interpret such information and how much weight to give to it. Questionnaire responses are no less constructions of reality than action plans, albeit constructed in a different and hopefully more focused way and for a different purpose. Although apparently giving more information about both process and outcomes, these data were intrinsically no more reliable or more readily understood on their own than that yielded by the analysis of the action plans. In contrast, the views of Chief Officers about the way in which the 'Tackling Offending' initiative had been managed were highly relevant to the issue of evaluation, highlighting deficiencies in the process of managing the initiative at a national level and making suggestions for the improvement of any future such initiatives which could not have been obtained in any other way, apart from face-to-face interviews.

These empirical measures therefore painted a picture which yielded tantalising glimpses of a different level of reality which could only be tapped through the detailed work in the two case study areas. In each area, a detailed programme of interviews was undertaken in order to generate additional qualitative data through which we sought to increase our understanding of both the processes at work and some of the outcomes. In order to test, for example, accounts of the consultation process, it was necessary to interview a number of probation officers and representatives of the key agencies identified in the 'Tackling Offending' initiative document, in order to gain some understanding of their perception and understanding of the process. Perhaps not surprisingly, these data qualified those from the other two main sources, confirming the importance of some of the questions raised above about how documentary sources, such as action plans, and more direct sources, such as questionnaire data, can and should be interpreted.

The interviews in the study areas also made it abundantly clear that evaluation studies cannot take place in some kind of phenomenological limbo and that any initiative, be it in the form of the 'Tackling Offending' initiative itself, or in the more tangible form of particular measures for direct intervention in the lives of offenders such as Intensive Probation (which was also part of the 'Tackling Offending' initiative), can only begin to be fully and effectively evaluated when understood in their organizational context (see also Mair et al., 1994). To make tenable judgements about the effectiveness of either process or outcome issues requires that the subject of the evaluation study is located in its social and organizational context, since not only will this have a profound impact on any criminal justice initiative, but without such contextual understanding, meaningful evaluation questions cannot be formulated.

As Pawson and Tilley have also argued in a recent critique of experimental approaches to evaluation studies, 'Programmes cannot be considered as some kind of external, impinging 'force' to which subjects 'respond'. Rather programmes 'work', *if subjects choose to make them work and are placed in the right conditions to enable them to do so*' (1994, p. 294 - italics in original). Thus the understandings and definitions of the key actors in any initiative are crucial in determining its success or failure in terms of both processes and outcomes because they are centrally involved in implementation.

In addition, and perhaps more importantly, their perspectives are also of central importance in defining what constitutes success or failure. They define these subjectively, for their own purposes and in their own terms, and their definitions may not necessarily accord with more 'objective' criteria. However, their subjective definitions may be more significant for those involved in the evaluation study, not only because these can have important consequences - for example, whether to continue with an initiative which they might regard as a failure - but also because their definitions may draw attention to criteria for evaluation which are more appropriate than externally defined, 'objective' criteria. In the context of the 'Tackling Offending' initiative, the key actors who were in a position to make the initiative work or not included chief officers of probation and social services departments, senior police officers, magistrates, Clerks to the Justices, probation officers and other social workers in the statutory and independent sectors.

In terms of 'objective' outcome criteria for the study, for the purpose of evaluating the impact of the 'Tackling Offending' initiative, it had been intended to draw upon both national and local statistical sources to examine its effect on the use of custody nationally and in each area. Early on in the research, however, it became apparent that little local data over and above that contained in the *Criminal Statistics Supplementary Tables (Volume 5)* were available, particularly in one of the study areas, and that such data would therefore be of limited value in undertaking an evaluation of outcomes. It was therefore decided that the programme of interviews would be supplemented by a detailed analysis of a sample of social inquiry reports (as they then were) and case records for each area relating to 17-20 year olds.

These documentary sources would reflect practice both before and after the initiative (in 1987 and 1990), and help to ascertain whether there was any evidence of changes in probation practice, both in terms of the information presented to courts and the actual practice of supervision. Such sources had the advantage of not being specifically formulated for either the 'Tackling Offending' initiative or for the purposes of the evaluation study, but suffered from the familiar disadvantage of being different kinds of accounts which, for differing reasons, had been constructed to present a particular version of reality for a specific purpose. Evaluative judgements made on these data were therefore, of necessity, inferential.

Each of the methods described above which were selected as part of the evaluation strategy for this study suffered from various shortcomings and none on its own would have been sufficiently robust to even begin to address some of the complex issues raised by any attempt to evaluate the 'Tackling Offending' initiative. Taken together, however, the methods represented a reasonably comprehensive, multi-faceted, multi-method approach which was able to address the complex range of issues and problems raised by such an evaluation study.

Criteria for failure or success

As argued above, the overall objectives of the initiative seemed fairly clear and the study was concerned to evaluate the formulation, implementation and effects of action plans on the use of custody for young adult offenders in each area. However, its objectives were often expressed in very general terms which were not always easily translated into criteria for empirical measurement. Thus, for example, taking the complex area of multi-agency working, it is not clear whether the Home Office intended that success should be judged in terms of the process and outcome of the establishment of organizational structures, such as inter-agency steering committees, or solely in terms of outcome measures such as actual diversionary achievements. This immediately draws attention to the failure of the Home Office to be clear about its own criteria for determining the success or failure of the initiative and the importance in any initiative, whether a policy or a practice initiative, to be clear from the outset about the terms in which success or failure should be measured.

In the absence of such criteria, researchers must construct their own criteria which are consistent with and can be sustained by the methodology employed. Since the nature and the emphasis of the 'Tackling Offending' initiative was on process issues, the criteria for evaluating the formulation of action plans also focused on these. Thus it was important to go beyond simply noting the claims made by areas of multi-agency consultation and involvement in the process of the formulation of their action plans and to gather specific information concerning the nature and extent of this. Assessing the results of the initiative in this respect required an evaluation of changes in inter-agency processes.

This was achieved through the use of the postal survey of all probation areas, which provided information about the process of consultation and any inter-agency structures to result from this. It was also achieved though the extensive programme of interviews in the case study areas, the aim of which was to build up a picture of respondents' perceptions and impressions of the process of the formulation and development of action plans in order to determine the extent to which they regarded themselves as having been involved in the process of formulation. By these means, the study was able to determine the extent to which the process objectives of the initiative had been met.

The issue of implementation also involved similar problems since the initiative was clearly concerned with both the process of implementation and the effects of the initiative - the specific intention was to develop a multi-agency approach to the planning, development and implementation of local action plans. At a national level, both the action plans and questionnaires were analysed to determine the extent to which action plans had been implemented as opposed to still being in the planning stage. Also with this in mind, questionnaires were circulated to all senior probation officers and probation officers in each study area, through which it was hoped to identify the most significant changes which had occurred as a result of the local action plan.

Unfortunately, the level of response to these questionnaires was disappointing and did not reveal the extent of information hoped for. Consequently, drawing on information gathered from the analysis of action plans, interviews were conducted in each study area with personnel involved with various schemes and initiatives to gather information about these and related organizational issues in order to determine the extent to which these had been the product of the 'Tackling Offending' initiative and to which action plans had been implemented. Of particular importance in evaluating this dimension of the initiative was the extent to which any measures which were a response to the 'Tackling Offending' initiative reflected multi-agency participation. Issues of both process and results were therefore also embodied in these criteria.

The main criterion for determining the extent to which the 'Tackling Offending' initiative was a success in terms of outcome - i.e. its impact on the use of custody for young offenders - was the conventional measure of recorded rates of imprisonment for offenders in this age group, some of the difficulties associated with which are outlined above. Because of these, it was also decided to seek complementary evidence of the impact of the 'Tackling Offending' initiative in the case study areas by looking for evidence of changes in probation practice, through social inquiry reports and records of supervision. Thus, in addition to drawing on such primary outcome data as were available, the evaluation also focused on secondary outcome data in the form of changes in probation practice.

The effects of the 'tackling offending' initiative

As noted above, the results of this study have been reported in detail elsewhere and will be reviewed here only in general terms in order to develop the arguments already outlined.

Formulation of action plans

The analysis of the action plans submitted to the Home Office indicated that just under half of all probation areas reported consultation with other agencies in formulating their action plans, although this did not necessarily mean that even these actions plans were jointly formulated. The postal questionnaire indicated a very high level of consultation within services, amongst staff at all levels, and that two thirds of probation services consulted with other statutory agencies, although consultation with independent sector agencies was more limited.

Over a third of those services which reported such consultations made use of an inter-agency group in this process and although some of these were formed as a specific response to the 'Tackling Offending' initiative, it was evident that a number made use of groups which were already in existence. It was also evident that whilst the large majority of areas reported involving sentencers in the process of formulating their action plans, this was largely through consultation in the context of probation committee meetings, etc., rather than a more substantive and integral involvement.

It also became clear that nearly half of all services had drafted their action plans on the basis of documented local strategies which were already in place at the time the 'Tackling Offending' initiative was launched, which suggested that these services were already some way down the road to achieving the objectives of the 'Tackling Offending' initiative and that they had therefore, to some extent, anticipated the initiative.

The interview programmes in the case study areas qualified this information in significant ways, however, and gave an insight into processes in the two areas studies which suggested that similar qualifications might be necessary in relation to other areas. For example, in both areas, local strategies were firmly in place before the 'Tackling Offending' initiative and there was a considerable reluctance on the part of senior probation managers in these areas to abandon the considerable organizational investment made in these existing strategies. These were therefore re-packaged to fit into the framework of the 'Tackling Offending' initiative, without substantive changes being made.

In addition, although both areas had inter-agency groups which acted as fora for the discussion of strategies for dealing with young offenders, both of these were already in existence at the time of the 'Tackling Offending' initiative and each operated differently in important respects which were not apparent from the other data collected. In one area, the group did indeed produce a joint strategy, although it was apparent that some agencies had felt excluded from the process of consultation, particularly in the early stages.

In the other area, the action plan was discussed with other agencies at the county inter-agency group and it was drafted in a way which took account of aspirations of working with other agencies, but there was in effect, no jointly formulated strategy or proposals for inter-agency initiatives. In this area, the inter-agency group was mainly a discussion forum and the main agencies which participated were protective of their organizational autonomy in a way which militated against the joint formulation of a local action plan, particularly within the short time scale provided by the 'Tackling Offending' initiative. Other research confirms that similar inter-agency initiatives have been affected by similar difficulties (Fraser et al., 1992).

Implementation of action plans

The action plans themselves were less valuable as a source of data about implementation, since they were by definition largely planning documents. However, they did provide information about certain aspects of the implementation of the 'Tackling Offending' initiative which was of use. For example, although many areas reported already making available certain of the services or facilities for young adult offenders required by the initiative, only just over two fifths of services reported using outside agencies in the management or implementation of their programmes and only three services reported having a multi-agency steering group responsible for the implementation of programmes as suggested in the 'Tackling Offending' initiative.

In the context of the 'Tackling Offending' initiative, the Home Office also required all services to undertake monitoring and evaluation of key aspects of the initiative. The action plans revealed that although just under three fifths of services reported undertaking general monitoring and evaluation, only two reported monitoring diversion from custody and only five reoffending rates, two of the main elements of the 'Tackling Offending' initiative. The results of the postal questionnaire confirmed this picture. Although some 80 per cent of services had full-time Research and Information Officers, their capacity to monitor the specific issues identified by the 'Tackling Offending' initiative was generally very limited.

The analysis of the postal questionnaire also indicated that over two thirds of services said that they provided specific initiatives for young adult offenders and that they had adhered to the time scale for implementing their action plans. However, only the minority of services provided information about the degree of implementation and it was clear that relatively few had implemented these completely.

Enquiries about implementation in the case study areas tended to confirm the picture presented by the other data - that probation services played the major role in implementation and that many of the initiatives for young offenders referred to in their action plans were already in place and available as a result of initiatives developed in the wake of the Criminal Justice Act, 1982 and the *Statement of National Objectives and Priorities* (Home Office, 1984), which had led to the development of local objectives and priorities.

National statistics indicated that by 1987, the use of custody for young adult offenders had already begun to decline and that this process gathered pace in 1988 and 1989. It is in this context that the majority of areas claimed that the measures which they had put in place in response to the 'Tackling Offending' initiative had reduced the use of custody for this age group, although less than half of all probation services were able to produce any evidence to support these claims and the statistics show that these alleged 'effects' actually pre-dated the implementation of measures introduced in response to the initiative.

Our case studies revealed that one area was indeed able to monitor the use of custody. In the other, however, there was no systematically provided information on local sentencing trends to enable the service to monitor the impact of the 'Tackling Offending' initiative and, in view of the failure of many areas to address this issue convincingly in either their action plans or their responses to the postal questionnaire, there is good cause to believe that this situation was not atypical of a number of other areas[1]. Our supplementary study of a sample of social inquiry reports and records of supervision in these areas also revealed little evidence of significant changes in practice in terms of the targeting of young adult offenders or of ensuring their participation in the kinds of programmes envisaged by the 'Tackling Offending' initiative.

Summary and conclusions - success or failure?

The data collected in the course of this evaluative study suggest that the 'Tackling Offending' initiative was only partially successful in achieving its objectives. In terms of both process and outcomes, although there was some increase in inter-agency collaboration in the formulation of action plans and in the provision of initiatives for young adult offenders, much of this was of less substance than the action plans themselves suggested and was a repackaging of work which was already in progress. There is also no way of attributing the fall in the use of custody, which subsequently became apparent but which was already beginning to occur before the 'Tackling Offending' initiative was launched, to the initiative itself.

However, as Mair et al. have argued:

> A process evaluation will show how an initiative was devised in the first place and the reasons for this; it will show how it was put into practice and whether or not this differed from the blueprint; it

will investigate developments over time and attempt to demonstrate why subsequent changes took place. By doing these things, a process evaluation provides the context in which outcome measures can be fully interpreted. (Mair et al., 1994, p. 8)

In terms of the broader objectives of the 'Tackling Offending' initiative, when viewed from this perspective our study of the processes at work reveals the complexities of organizational responses to attempts to influence the practice of criminal justice agencies through the means of such initiatives. Furthermore, although there was some evidence of a number of changes of the kind which were sought by the initiative, it is even less clear that these were caused by the 'Tackling Offending' initiative itself.

This study not only confirms the value for both researchers and policy-makers of the distinction that has been drawn between process and outcome evaluation but suggests the need for a closer examination of the relationship between the two. A very simple model of this relationship could cross-tabulate the achievements of process objectives against outcome objectives (see Figure 4.1), recognising explicitly that process objectives might be achieved without the desired objectives, or alternatively that outcome objectives might be achieved without the intervening process changes.

		Outcome Objectives Achieved	
		Yes	No
Process Objectives Achieved	Yes	1	3
	No	2	4

Figure 4.1: Process v outcome evaluations: a simplified model

The evidence from this study complicates the model further, by suggesting that the achievement of process objectives may be only partial and not necessarily directly attributable to the initiative in question. Similarly the achievement of outcome objectives may not be solely or mainly attributable to the process changes associated with the initiative.

Typically, criminal justice initiatives are both products of and influences upon the current penal policy environment. Many of the changes of practice that the 'Tackling Offending' initiative aimed to bring about (e.g. in terms of sentencing and probation service practice) were already in train at the time of its announcement. To that extent, it reflected an emerging climate of professional opinion and behaviour, for which it then served as an added stimulus. Even if some of its detailed process objectives were not achieved it might nevertheless have made a significant, symbolic and instrumental, contribution to the achievement of change in process and outcome.

Finally, this study, which sought to use a multi-method approach to evaluation involving the triangulation of different sets of data collected by using a range of methods (see Hammersley and Atkinson, 1993), also demonstrates the value of moving beyond simple indicators of outcome, particularly in attempts to evaluate policy initiatives such as this. The study by Mair et al. (1994) of Intensive Probation, which was also part of the 'Tackling Offending' initiative, confirms many of our conclusions about the initiative and the significance of many of the issues we have outlined above. As he argued several years earlier:

> For the most part, the idea that ... agents of criminal justice have views about their work, are likely to have views about any new developments which will have an impact on their normal working practice - and that they may well be involved in putting such developments into practice - that these views may have an effect upon practice, and that all of these factors could have a crucial influence upon the outcome of any new initiative; all of these facts are significant by their absence from evaluative studies (with a few partial exceptions). (Mair, 1990, p. 4)

Much research and evaluation is method driven - the phenomena being studied are too often moulded and 'squeezed' into the shape required in order to make them susceptible to examination through the research methods chosen. The evaluation of any criminal justice initiative which fails to acknowledge this tendency and to develop methodologies and research strategies which take adequate account of processes as well as outcomes can only ever provide, at the best, partial answers to the key questions. Although fuller answers are inevitably less clear-cut and more complicated, and this is something which is not always welcomed by policy makers, it can surely no longer be acceptable to settle for anything less, in this field of study perhaps above all others.

Note 1. It is interesting to note that subsequent Government expenditure plans for law and order emphasised *inter alia* the need for the probation service to provide 'tough and demanding community penalties, where appropriate, and to provide the courts with the service they require' and make 'provision for a substantial information systems programme to help the service meet these goals'.

(Home Office News Release 241/94, 29 November 1994*)*.

References

Bottomley, A.K., James, A.L., Bochel, C. and Robinson, D-M. (1992), *A Study of the Probation Service Response to the 'Tackling Offending' Initiative,* Centre for Criminology and Criminal justice, University of Hull.

Bottomley, A.K., James, A.L., Bochel, C. and Robinson, D-M. (1993), 'The probation service response to the 'Tackling Offending' initiative, *Home Office Research Bulletin, 33,* 18-24.

Fraser, P., Bottomley, A.K. and James, A.L. (1992), *An Evaluation of Area Accommodation Strategies: A Study of the Impact of Home Office Circular 35/88, Review of Non-Custodial Offender Accommodation - A Research Report,* Association of Chief Officers of Probation, Wakefield.

Hammersley, M. and Atkinson, P. (1983), *Ethnography: Principles in Practice,* Tavistock, London.

Home Office (1984), *Probation Service in England and Wales: Statement of National Objectives and Priorities,* Home Office, London.

Home Office (1988a), *Punishment, Custody and the Community,* HMSO, London.

Home Office (1988b), *Tackling Offending: An Action Plan,* Home Office, London.

James, A.L. and Bottomley, A.K. (1994), 'Probation Partnerships Revisited', *The Howard Journal of Criminal Justice, 33.*

Mair, G. (1989), 'Some Developments in Probation in the 1980's', *Home Office Research Bulletin, 27,* 33-6.

Mair, G. (1994), 'Evaluating the effects of diversion strategies on the attitudes and practices of agents of the criminal justice system', Nineteenth Criminological Research Conference, Council of Europe - *New Social Strategies and the Criminal Justice System*, Strasbourg.

Mair, G., Lloyd, C., Nee, C. and Sibbitt, R. (1994), *Intensive Probation in England and Wales: An Evaluation*, Home Office Research Study No. 133, Home Office, London.

Pawson, R. and Tilley, N. (1994) 'What Works in Evaluation Research?', *British Journal of Criminology, 34,* (3).

5 Evaluating intensive probation

George Mair

Intensive probation (IP) was a major policy initiative launched by the Home Office in the late 1980s, Essentially, it took some of the ideas of IP schemes which had swept across the USA from the beginning of the decade and tried to apply these to probation in England and Wales. In the USA, certainly towards the start of the intensive probation movement, reports stressed the success of this new approach to working with offenders in the community. It was only a matter of time before the achievements of IP came to the notice of the Home Office and a decision was made to try to replicate its success in England and Wales.

In this paper, I will describe the origins of IP in this country, the approach to evaluating it which was followed and the reasons for this, briefly set out the key findings of the evaluation, and reflect upon the methodology used. It is always easier with hindsight to see the advantages and disadvantages of what one has done, and in a sense this paper is an effort to explain how the evaluation could have been done better.

Intensive probation

Various forms of 'intensive probation' have been practiced in England and Wales, the most famous being the IMPACT experiment (Intensive Matched Probation and After-Care Treatment) which took place in the first half of the seventies. This project represented the culmination of work which had begun in what was then the Home Office Research Unit ten years earlier, a considerable amount of resources were devoted to it, and a detailed study was carried out of its effects (see Folkard et al., 1974,1976). Whether expectations for IMPACT were too high, the methodology for the research was inappropriate, the programme itself was not well-founded, or for other reasons, the conclusions of the study were that IMPACT was a failure. It did not help that the second volume of the study was published in 1976 immediately after Stephen Brody's *The Effectiveness of Sentencing* which was seen as further confirmation of the 'Nothing Works' notion which had recently taken root in the USA (see Martinson, 1974, and Lipton et al., 1975).

The 'new' IP movement is rather different from previous versions. Previously, intensive meant that more of the same was meted out to offenders - more social work, more counselling, more help. Today, intensive means more rigorous and demanding; offenders are required to be seen by probation officers more often, they have extra conditions attached to their probation order, they are subject to increased surveillance. In the USA, those subject to intensive probation are bound by a wide variety of conditions which can include community service, a curfew (often electronically monitored), employment or school attendance requirements, checks of police arrest records, urinalysis, restitution, and payment of fees to offset the costs of supervision. At a time when the law-and-order agenda in general was increasingly becoming dominated by the political right, such an emphasis on the control and surveillance of offenders was obviously attractive to the government.

IP's origins were many and various. In the first place, prison overcrowding was a key factor although the main target group for IP (17-20 year olds with custodial sentences of up to 18 months) had been a steadily decreasing part of the prison population since 1985 (Home Office, 1992a). Indeed, IP can be seen as yet another - and possibly the last - of the many post-war initiatives introduced in an attempt to tackle the crisis of prison overcrowding: attendance centres, community service orders, the suspended sentence, parole, probation centres, probation hostels, bail information schemes.

Two other themes which lay behind the introduction of IP were the need for effective punishment and the necessity of restoring judicial confidence in the work of the probation service. Partly no doubt as a result of the increasing costs of imprisonment and the high reconviction rates associated with custody, prison was being perceived as a not particularly effective punishment for many offenders:

Imprisonment is not the most effective punishment for most crime. Custody should be reserved as punishment for very serious offences, especially when the offender is violent and a continuing risk to the public. But not every sentencer or member of the public has full confidence in the present orders which leave offenders in the community. (Home Office, 1988a)

But if offenders were to be diverted from custody, then effective punishment in the community was required and there was a nagging feeling that the probation service was not quite as effective as it might be. The Audit Commission (1989) report on the probation service was particularly important in bringing this point to the fore, as it argued that the increase in the use of probation and community service during the 80s had been at the expense of the fine which meant that far from reducing the use of custody it had led to increases in the numbers imprisoned. Closely linked with the idea of effective punishment was the notion that sentencers had lost the trust they had had in the probation service (this is implied in the final sentence of the above quote). This idea floated about a lot in the late 80s but without any evidence to substantiate it; in fact, there was no evidence that such trust had ever existed or that it had now disappeared.

There was also the glowing example of the considerable decrease in juvenile involvement in the criminal justice system to try to emulate; this showed that what might have seemed to be an intractable problem could be overcome. Between 1980 and 1990, the number of juveniles proceeded against in the magistrates' courts fell from 139,000 to 54,000 (Home Office, 1992b). Part of the reason for such a drop was demographic - the number of juveniles in the population was decreasing - and IP could well ride this demographic wave as it filtered through to the 17-20 age group. But there was a naive assumption that whatever had worked for juveniles (and this was a question which was not easily answered, but which did not seem to be a result of direct governmental intervention) would work for the 17-20 year olds. The latter are much more likely to suffer from unemployment, homelessness, they may be married with children, and are more likely to be involved in the misuse of drugs or alcohol.

Costs also played a role in the origins of IP. Prison is a very expensive way of dealing with offenders and if cheaper and equally (or possibly more) effective methods of dealing with offenders could be found this would be a desirable outcome. In comparison to other community penalties, IP promised to be expensive - but not as expensive as custody. A key factor in cost effectiveness would be successful targeting: if IP did not act to divert offenders from a custodial sentence but acted as a supplementary community sentence, then any cost advantage would be lost. Research into the Medway Close Support Unit (a progenitor of intensive supervision for young offenders) found that the cost per day of the Unit was less than that for a detention centre, but the length of sentence at the Unit was twice as long as a detention centre order, making the cost per sentence of the Unit twice as high (Ely et al., 1987).

The example of IP in the USA was undoubtedly a key background factor. Prison overcrowding, saving money, and reducing reoffending were usually cited as the main aims of IP programmes in America. Initial research tended to be enthusiastic about the effectiveness of IP in achieving such aims (see e.g. Erwin, 1987; Pearson, 1987), but later studies have raised questions about just how far IP schemes have succeeded in these terms (see the articles in Byrne, Lurigio and Petersilia, 1992). Indeed, Michael Tonry (1990) has argued that while IP programmes fail to achieve their stated goals, they succeed admirably in achieving a series of latent goals:

> They serve bureaucratic and organizational goals by enabling probation administrators to be 'tough on crime' and thereby increase the institutional and political credibility of probation. This brings more staff, more money, and new programs to probation. They serve administrators' normative goals. By being purposely more punitive than traditional probation, ISP programs permit administrators to express a reduced tolerance of crime and disorder that they share with the general public and political leaders.... They serve professional and psychological goals. By attracting new resources and new visibility, ISP programs put probation on the front lines of crime control and thereby enhance the esteem accorded probation and vicariously, the professional and personal self-esteem of probation officers.

One final factor which lay behind the origins of IP was the unspoken desire by the government to change probation culture. Increasingly during the 1980s the probation service had been subject to changes which had - directly and indirectly - led to greater accountability for its work (Mair, 1996). To exaggerate (though only slightly), many Conservative politicians tended to see probation officers as soft on criminals and wanted to toughen up probation; some of this view is captured in the words of John Patten when he was Minister of State at the Home Office:

> Some people in the Probation Service seem to have a hang-up about language and do not like to be involved in things like punishment, nor perhaps sometimes to regard themselves as part of the criminal justice system. (Probation Journal, 1988)

Culture change was certainly not an explicit factor in IP, but there can be little doubt that introducing IP was part of the process of toughening up the probation service and making it more 'punitive'.

A wide variety of background factors, then, lay behind the introduction of IP; so what did the initial plans for IP programmes look like ? Preliminary ideas about IP can be perceived in the 1988 Green Paper *Punishment,*

Custody and the Community (Home Office, 1988a), but the first specific proposals appeared in a document which appeared later in the year *Tackling Offending: an action plan* (Home Office, 1988b):

> Probation services in selected areas should set up *'intensive probation' programmes* exclusively for offenders who would otherwise receive custodial sentences. The courts should be involved closely in the design of the programmes and the police should be kept in touch. The projects should be *monitored, costed and evaluated.* (emphasis in original)

IP schemes were expected to target 17-20 year old offenders who were at risk of a custodial sentence; they were to provide a degree of control over offenders with frequent reporting to probation officers, and to be based around a probation centre or specified activities requirement. Other key elements of IP schemes were: rigorous referral and selection procedures in order to avoid the risk of net-widening and ensure that lower risk offenders were subjected to less intensive forms of supervision; a comprehensive and individualised programme to be worked out with each offender and presented to the court; a focus on confronting offending behaviour in the programme; the use of a multi-agency approach was encouraged so that the skills and experience of voluntary and other statutory agencies might be utilised; and monitoring and evaluation was to be built in, including some assessment of the participation of ethnic minority and female offenders.

Given the variety of background factors, the somewhat vague nature of the guidelines drawn up by the Home Office, and the fact that IP was intended as an experimental initiative, a simple research design concentrating on recidivism was out of the question.

The evaluation methodology

Although the bottom line for the success or failure of a court sentence for the Home Office remains the reconviction rate (despite the various problems associated with such a measure - see Chapter 3 in this volume), other possible measures of success have been discussed (see Mair, 1991). The nature of the IP initiative and its early development prior to schemes taking offenders, offered an opportunity to test out some ideas about how sentences of the court could be more appropriately evaluated. Even at the initial stages of discussion and negotiation with probation services, it was clear that a smooth and consistent path for developing IP schemes was unlikely. For example, there was confusion about how (or indeed whether) the IP initiative fitted into the proposals in the *Tackling Offending* document. Most of the ten Chief Probation Officers approached about setting up IP schemes were apprehensive. They argued that having taken on board the *Tackling Offending* proposals and spent time planning developments with staff and sentencers, there would be confusion and scepticism if they were to go back and say that there was a further raft of ideas which they wanted to take forward. The six month gap between issuing *Tackling Offending* and following up its more marginal proposals for IP was not long enough for the two initiatives to be sufficiently differentiated from each other.

Such factors are rarely discussed when evaluating court sentences - the focus on reconviction rates tends to preclude studying how these (or any other outcome measures) are produced. And yet without such work, reconviction rates on their own are practically useless as a measure of effectiveness. A simple reconviction rate is almost impossible to interpret without a good deal of further knowledge. Is a reconviction rate of 75 per cent, for example, indicative of success or failure? Lacking more information, it is very much a matter of opinion - and decisions can be made about the continuation or termination of the disposal in question on such flimsy grounds. A rate of 75 per cent might be judged a success if the sentence had achieved its aim of targeting very high risk offenders, had calculated predicted reconviction rates for its offenders which were higher than those actually found, and was not consuming a disproportionate amount of resources. On the other hand, 75 per cent would rightly be judged a failure if the project had not captured its intended target group and instead had been dealing with relatively low risk offenders whose predicted reconviction rate was lower than that found.

But even with such information it would still be difficult to replicate the project if it was a success, or make sure that its failures were not repeated. To do this, a process evaluation is necessary. Essentially, this would study how the project was devised in the policy stages, how it was transmitted to practitioners, how it was put into practice, and how it developed over time. With this information, it becomes possible to place reconviction rates and other measures of effectiveness in a context and interpret them more fully. It becomes possible to discern the reasons for success and consider how these might be taken into account in future; and the reasons for failure are clearer, which should help to ensure that these are avoided in future. Process evaluation is not a luxury option to be added into an evaluation study, but a vital prerequisite to understanding where outcomes come from.

The evaluation of IP involved a process evaluation as well as an outcome evaluation. The process evaluation involved choosing three IP areas as case studies (Durham, Leeds and the West Midlands). Researchers visited the areas over a 24 month period to study the implementation and development of IP; they talked to the probation officers involved, observed supervision sessions, and - on occasion - participated in some sessions. The three case studies were not intended to be comparative nor were they representative of IP. IP was very much an experimental development and areas had a good deal of discretion in how they went about planning and setting up IP schemes. Durham was chosen because it was a small area and was setting up its IP scheme from scratch; West Yorkshire because it had two IP schemes which had been running for some time before the official start date; and the West Midlands because it was a large metropolitan area starting IP from scratch. By talking informally with the key players in IP, the researchers were able to amass a great deal of information about how it was working on the ground and the micro-politics of the schemes.

For the outcome evaluation, several outcome measures were to be considered. Reconviction rates were included, of course, but it was important to try to move away from the simple yes/no approach to recidivism where reconviction equals failure and non-reconviction equals success. Thus, we proposed to look at: reconviction during the course of IP supervision as well as during subsequent normal supervision; the time to reconviction; the offence for which offenders were reconvicted; and their sentence on reconviction. Other outcome measures were diversion from custody, financial costs, the views of sentencers, and the views of offenders. These five were seen as primary measures, but after discussion with the probation services involved in IP it was decided to add secondary measures which could be specific to IP schemes or the individualised programmes put together for offenders. For example, they might cover help with accommodation, employment or drug misuse.

In addition to the fieldwork carried out, basic information was collected on all those referred to IP programmes, recommended for IP in a social inquiry report, or sentenced to IP from all participating areas for the duration of the project (1 April 1990 - 31 March 1992) at three times: at the time of sentence, at the conclusion of the period on IP, and at the end of the period of normal supervision.

To elicit the views of sentencers, a mail questionnaire was sent to all magistrates in the three case study areas. Unfortunately, it proved impossible to follow the same method for distributing the questionnaires in each area. In some Petty Sessional Divisions the justices' clerk asked for a specific number of questionnaires and passed these on to their magistrates; in others, the researchers were given a name but the clerk passed the questionnaire on to the individual concerned, while in others the questionnaire was mailed direct to magistrates. A low response rate to the questionnaire was expected in any event, but these different approaches used in distribution meant that it was impossible to carry out follow-ups to boost the response rate.

The main findings of the study[1]

As was expected from the outset, it was difficult to talk about IP in general terms as schemes differed widely. Instead of the ten projects which had been envisaged, only eight were implemented in one form or another. One area dropped out prior to the start of the initiative. Some schemes had been operating prior to the official introduction of IP on 1 April 1990, while others took some months to get off the ground. Indeed, one IP scheme failed to start during the two year period of the initiative; while another only ran for 12 months before closing down. Thus only seven schemes can be said to have participated fully in the IP experiment. Some schemes were based upon existing probation centres (then known as 4B requirements), while others made use of specified activities requirements (4A), and one - departing completely from Home Office guidelines - was based upon voluntary attendance. Naturally, therefore, the various schemes ended up with different kinds of offenders being referred to them as Table 5.1 shows.

Overall, during the 24 months of the experiment a total of 1,677 offenders were referred for intensive probation and, as might be expected, the great majority were male (95 per cent). Around half were aged between 17 and 20, had six or more previous convictions and had previous experience of custody; while almost two-thirds were sentenced at the Crown Court. The most common offence was burglary (42 per cent), with theft (16 per cent) and violent offences (14 per cent) also fairly common. In general, these figures suggest that IP schemes were successfully targeting offenders who were at high risk of a custodial sentence, but they hide considerable variations amongst areas.

It is notable that some areas were more successful than others at targeting those at risk of custody; Hampshire, Gwent, Leeds and Durham tended to be better in this regard than the West Midlands, Berkshire and Northumbria (ignoring Manchester with only 17 offenders) . The reasons for such differences in IP schemes lie in the design and objectives of the schemes: some focused on the Crown Court while others did not, some aimed at 17-20 year olds exclusively, while others spread their net more widely. One area - Northumbria - was responsible for almost half the female referrals as it had made a conscious decision to design IP modules which catered for female offenders.

Table 5.1
The characteristics of offenders referred to IP schemes

Area	Number of referrals	% male	% 17-20	% Crown Court	% 6+ prev convictions	% prev custody
Berkshire	94	94	88	60	35	32
Durham	95	98	52	50	61	67
Gwent	186	99	36	55	68	68
Hampshire	351	98	40	85	63	62
Leeds	532	97	47	73	50	58
M'chester	17	88	82	35	59	65
Northumb.	215	81	35	39	43	38
W. Mids.	187	96	86	47	29	41
Total No.	1,677	95	50	64	51	54

Sentencer satisfaction with IP was high, although it must be added that there was little agreement about where IP fitted into the sentencing options available and precisely what its objectives were. In general, the advantages of IP were seen as system-oriented (i.e. it would lead to a reduction in the numbers being sentenced to custody) or welfare-oriented (it would rehabilitate offenders); it was rare for any punitive aspects of IP to be mentioned. Overwhelmingly, the major potential disadvantage of IP was identified as the possibility that offenders or the general public might see it as a soft option. Interestingly, the process of sending questionnaires to magistrates stimulated interest in IP as some responses noted that they had not heard of it prior to receiving the questionnaire.

We were interested in the views of probation officers about IP for two reasons. First, in the USA there was increasing evidence that IP schemes had created some dissatisfaction in probation agencies as IP officers were perceived as an elite (and, indeed, in many cases were paid more than their counterparts in 'normal' probation). And second, if probation staff were unhappy with IP this would have an impact upon the schemes themselves; for example, those working on schemes could be unenthusiastic and uninterested, while non-IP staff could refuse to refer potential offenders to schemes. In the event, probation staff who worked on IP schemes were enthusiastic about them (with the exception of those in one case study area), although this was almost certainly due to the fact that they were specially recruited for the task and therefore interested in running more intensive supervision programmes. In one case study area the introduction of IP was not well handled; the area had an agenda of its own which did not quite fit that of the Home Office, the implementation of IP was confused, and IP itself was seen as just window-dressing.

Non-IP staff were not quite so enthusiastic about IP, but this was dependant upon how long schemes had been running and the degree of consultation which had taken place. It became clear during the course of the research that there were considerable advantages in having an IP scheme which had been up and running rather than planning, designing and implementing one to try to fit into the timetable of the initiative. With the former, most of the opposition had been dealt with, worries had been smoothed over, and staff had seen that IP was not 'the end of probation as we know it'. With the latter, however, all of these issues had to be gone through, sometimes in considerable detail. Negative comments about IP focused on the fact that it was elitist; on the claim that more resources had been made available to IP when the same ends could have been achieved by ordinary probation orders; and on the use of voluntary organisations whose staff were seen as unqualified and questions about the enforcement of orders were raised.

As proposed in the Home Office guidelines, all IP areas made use of voluntary organisations to a greater or lesser extent. But there was apprehension about this aspect of IP, as during the initiative the Home Office issued discussion documents which floated the idea of the increasing involvement of voluntary organisations in the supervision of offenders. Many probation officers saw this as a way of marginalising the probation service and therefore there was far more suspicion about the use of outside agencies than there might have been.

The views of offenders were remarkably positive (although it should be noted that it proved very difficult to fix appointments to talk to them). Many probation officers seemed to think that IP would prove to be too demanding for offenders and that they would rebel against the rigorous requirements expected of them. If anything, however, offenders seemed to enjoy the attention which was paid to them as part of intensive supervision; they did not appear to find the demands of IP particularly onerous. This was reflected in the surprisingly positive comments made about their project workers who were, for the most part, not professionally qualified probation officers. The project workers loomed large in the life of offenders during their time on IP and their efforts on the behalf of offenders were appreciated. Unfortunately, there was some evidence that offenders perceived their probation officers as not very helpful - perhaps because during IP they did not play such a prominent part for offenders as did project workers.

Reflections on the methodology

Perhaps the key question to be asked of the approach used to evaluate the IP initiative is whether, with hindsight, I would do the same again. In general terms, the answer is yes but this is not to say that there is no scope for improvement.

Overall, the evaluation methodology worked well. The research involved a great deal of hard work on the part of the researchers who collected considerable amounts of data; the study would have been enriched if they could have spent more time in the three case study areas but as is the norm with work in the Research and Planning Unit, this project was only one of several that they were involved with. But our focus on process provided material which, although seemingly simplistic, tended to be ignored or taken for granted by policy makers and probation managers - yet played critical roles in the development and implementation of the IP policy (which, of course, had effects on the outcomes of IP).

The confusion over IP's status in relation to the 'Tackling Offending' initiative did not help in clarifying what IP was all about. The relatively vague guidelines (which could be ignored with impunity as one service demonstrated) allowed probation services scope to use discretion in designing their IP schemes, but there was surprisingly little evidence of innovation in IP programmes. Timescales were unworkable: some areas already had IP schemes up and running, some could not start until some months after the official commencement date, and as noted above, one area dropped its IP scheme after 12 months while another could not begin during the 24 months of the initiative. Central policy was also unhelpful in its timing over pronouncements about the role of voluntary organisations in the supervision of offenders, and about the introduction of the combination order. The former led to suspicion among probation officers that the probation service was going to lose its position in the supervision of offenders to such organisations; while the proposals for the combination order led to many of those involved in IP schemes wondering how IP would relate to the new order. The lack of innovation in IP schemes was worrying; was this due to unwillingness or inability to design innovative programmes; was it due to the fact that the timescale for IP was not long enough; was it due to lack of resources; how far was it due to fear of failure and yet the desire to be seen to comply with Home Office demands? Decisions about the form of IP schemes seemed to be taken without any consideration of the possible repercussions: a brand new scheme based in one locality with a dedicated group of staff would have the problems of any such new scheme but at least would have a clear identity; a general scheme which simply changed titles and tinkered with procedures could lead to confusion and uncertainty amongst staff (and one of the case study areas was an excellent example of this).

The project failed to collect adequate data on the financial costs of IP. In one case study area where data were available the costs of IP were found to be considerably more than that of other community penalties, but less than a comparable custodial sentence of five months. At the time of the research, few probation areas were in a position to supply information about the costs of specific aspects of their work although this is expected to change as financial management systems are implemented.

We also failed completely to collect data on what we referred to as secondary outcome measures such as help with employment, drug misuse, accommodation, etc. There is no doubt that all of the areas held such information, but it was not in a form which was easily accessible to researchers. If we had had more resources, we could have used researchers to spend time going through IP offenders' files, but this was not feasible. A study currently underway under the direction of Professor Mike Hough at South Bank University is piloting various methods of using 'needs' scales in probation and, if successful, would make the collection of such data a much simpler exercise.

How useful is such a study to Home Office policy makers and to probation staff? There is a great deal of what is usually condescendingly referred to as 'soft' data in the IP evaluation - not a format which is favoured by policy makers. However, the kind of material discussed in the previous paragraphs should be helpful in planning future initiatives; try not to float them when other proposals are around, clarify the objectives of the scheme, etc. The big question, of course, is just how far government takes note of research it has commissioned. As for probation managers, there is a tendency for them to welcome research if it shows their service in a good light, but to ignore it if it suggests failure. One of the main aims of the IP evaluation, was not simply to assess success or failure but to try to explain how that had come about. If a successful outcome cannot be explained then it is almost impossible to replicate, and if failure cannot be explained then how do we guard against repeated failure? No-one likes to fail, but with new projects failure must be a possibility and those with a stake in the project should be prepared for failure, ready to learn from it and prepared to try again. With the methodology used here, it should be an easier matter to identify where and why failure occurs.

The IP initiative was ideal for an evaluation of the kind described; it was experimental, developing, messy, and involved various groups and agencies (this could almost serve as a description of the evaluation itself). As I have tried to show, the study was by no means as neat and tidy as we would have liked and it involved considerable resources. Having said that, however, the advantages of such an approach outweigh the drawbacks. The need for process studies to set outcomes in their full organisational and structural context cannot be under-estimated and should be encouraged wherever possible.

Note

1. For a full description of the findings of the IP evaluation see Mair et al. (1994)

References

'A "new world of punishment": the view from John Patten's window of opportunity', *Probation Journal* (1988), *35*, 81-84.

Audit Commission (1989), *The Probation Service: promoting value for money*, HMSO, London.

Brody, S. (1976), *The Effectiveness of Sentencing: a review of the literature*, Home Office Research Study No.35, HMSO, London.

Byrne, J.M., Lurigio, A.J. and Petersilia, J. (eds.) (1992), *Smart Sentencing: the emergence of intermediate sanctions*, Sage, Newbury Park.

Ely, P., Swift, A. and Sunderland, A. (1987), *Control Without Custody ? Non-custodial control of juvenile offenders*, Scottish Academic Press, Edinburgh.

Erwin, B. (1987), *Evaluation of Intensive Probation Supervision in Georgia: Final report*, Department of Corrections, Atlanta.

Folkard, M.S. et al. (1974), *IMPACT Vol.I: the design of the probation experiment and an interim evaluation*, Home Office Research Study No.24, HMSO, London.

Folkard et al. (1976), *IMPACT Vol.II: the results of the experiment*, Home Office Research Study No.36, HMSO, London.

Home Office (1988a), *Punishment, Custody and the Community*, Cm 424, HMSO, London.

Home Office (1988b), *Tackling Offending: an action plan*, Home Office, London.

Home Office (1992a), *Prison Statistics England and Wales 1990*, Cm 1800, HMSO, London..

Home Office (1992b), *Criminal Statistics England and Wales 1990*, Cm 1935, HMSO, London.

Lipton, D., Martinson, R. and Wilks, J. (1975), *The Effectiveness of Correctional Treatment: a survey of treatment evaluation studies*, Praeger, New York.

Mair, G. (1991), 'What works - nothing or everything ? Measuring the effectiveness of sentences', *Home Office Research Bulletin, 30*, 3-8.

Mair, G. (1996), 'Developments in probation in England and Wales 1984-1993', in G. McIvor (ed.) *Working with Offenders*, Jessica Kingsley, London.

Martinson, R. (1974), 'What Works ? Questions and answers about prison reform', *The Public Interest, 10*, 22-54.

Pearson, F. (1987), *Research on New Jersey's Intensive Supervision Program: Final report to the National Institute of Justice*, National Institute of Justice, Washington, DC.

Tonry, M. (1990), 'Stated and latent features of ISP', *Crime and Delinquency, 36*, 174-191.

6 Evaluating Scottish special probation schemes

Bryan Williams and Anne Creamer

Introduction

This chapter concerns the evaluation of what were at the time four experimental probation schemes in Scottish mainland regional authorities (Creamer, Hartley and Williams, 1992a). The Scottish context for the provision of such initiatives differs from elsewhere in the U.K. in that probation and other related functions are carried out within local authority Social Work Departments which also carry responsibility for all aspects of personal social service provision. This situation has pertained since the implementation of the Social Work Scotland Act 1968 and remains so despite a number of more recent changes in the funding and organisation of social work services within criminal justice. These include the introduction of 100 per cent funding arrangements whereby the local authorities act as agencies of central government, and the formulation and dissemination of National Standards and Objectives in 1991. These recent steps have sought to bring about greater consistency of service standards and clarity about the organisational and management arrangements within which functions like assessment for, and the supervision of, probation orders is carried out. Nonetheless, it remains the case that the local authorities, with their respective political mandates, carry the main responsibility for the design of services, the definition of service priorities and the maintenance of standards. This diversity will be further exemplified in April 1996 when the functions of the existing nine Regional mainland authorities are taken over by twenty-nine new unitary authorities.

The distinctive features of the Scottish criminal justice context may be disputed but it is widely agreed that it has been easier to retain a strong social welfare orientation to work within the court setting. The Sheriff Courts deal with a larger range of matters than any single court level in England and Wales and sheriffs sit in both summary jurisdiction and in indictable cases.

Individual sheriffs thus have a considerable influence on how justice is carried out in practice and social workers tend to become very sensitised to signs of approval or displeasure from the Bench. The range of sentencing options is somewhat more restricted in Scotland, lacking the type of semi-custodial options available elsewhere, and this tends to lead to more of a sentencing dichotomy in which custody acts as a measuring rod of seriousness. Traditionally, the Scottish courts have not fostered such close working relations with social workers as has been common with probation officers although this aspect is beginning to change in some areas.

The study reported on was part of a four year research project funded by the Scottish Office. The first phase of the study ran in parallel with a second project conducted at Glasgow University (Ford, Ditton and Laybourn, 1992) and really constituted the first attempt to document Scottish probation practice. From this first phase some interesting features emerged in respect of the type of cases recommended for, and subsequently given, probation orders and the issues typically concentrated on within probation supervision (Williams, Creamer and Hartley, 1988, 1990.) A previous study (Williams and Creamer, 1987) had found that there was a wide variation in the use of probation by the Scottish courts, with a small number of areas in which what has now become known as 'high tariff probation' was relatively common, if not frequent practice. This obviously involved the acceptance of the appropriateness of this course of action by both the authors of court reports and the courts themselves. In other areas probation was fairly exclusively reserved for less serious cases in which significant social needs had been identified. Practice in the former areas tended to be associated with lower than average custody rates[1] which could not easily be accounted for in terms of the nature of the area in which the court was situated or the types of case coming before it.

A literature review conducted by the authors prior to the commencement of the study suggested that an adequate statement of the aims of probation would need to include the following:

1. The provision of appropriate help to offenders.
2. Social control through supervision and surveillance.
3. The containment of an individual's offending during the currency of the order.
4. The reduction of the individual's offending in the future.
5. The prevention of crime.
6. The diversion of offenders from custody.

Measures of individual outcome, whether reconviction rates or some other measure of satisfaction, do not provide adequate criteria for judgements about the effectiveness of probation in the wider sentencing context (particularly relating to the diversionary aim 6 above) and it was decided, therefore, to focus the research on what might be termed the *'macro'* aspects rather than to repeat other individual outcome studies. This evaluation of probation innovations thus concentrated on the extent to which they achieved the aim of *diverting* serious offenders from custody by creating a new and credible community disposal for use by the Scottish courts.

The authors also conducted a parallel qualitative study designed to explore the processes by which the projects came into being and the levels of satisfaction expressed by various stake-holders as to their evolution and outcomes (Creamer, Hartley and Williams, 1992b).

Aims of the research

The main aim of the study was to investigate the impact of a limited number of the first experimental probation schemes to emerge within Scotland; to measure their effectiveness in diverting people from custody; and to assess the impact of their introduction on other non-custodial disposals, notably community service and standard probation. As part of this aim it was planned to monitor the extent to which social workers were willing to recommend these new provisions for serious offenders and the corresponding willingness of sentencers to accede to such recommendations in the most serious cases. These objectives were pursued within an action research orientation in which researchers worked closely with service managers and project staff to develop clear criteria defining eligibility and suitability for the various projects. Through involvement of this kind it was hoped also to assist in developing new channels of communication with the courts and to improve clarity of decision making, particularly concerning the use of probation orders. The parallel qualitative study was designed to investigate and report on the processes through which the projects were brought into being and to draw conclusions as to which factors were most likely to be significant in terms of the future viability and sustainability of the schemes studied.

Methodology

The probation schemes which were finally included within the scope of the research were identified by sending letters to all the chief officers throughout mainland Scotland asking them to identify new probation projects in their region which were considered innovative and which might be considered to have an impact on the use by courts of community based sanctions. An important pre-condition was the willingness of project staff and managers to engage with the action research. In the event four such schemes emerged which represented, at the time, the main developments within Scottish probation. These are described in more detail below.

In each research site, a one-year retrospective study of social enquiry reports (SERs) was carried out for the period immediately preceding the commencement of the project or initiative. The data derived from the content analysis was used to establish baselines for social work practice and for local sentencing patterns against which subsequent changes could be measured (known as the *retrospective sample*.) The number of cases (SERs) involved at this stage were: Muirville (283); Cambusneal (521); Duncansburgh (206); Rutherton (141).

Once the probation schemes were operational a content analysis was carried out on the SERs prepared by all the social work teams referring cases to them during the research period which was divided into two phases (known as the *current study* - phases 1 and 2) Information was routinely recorded on:

1. The nature and gravity of the offences charged;
2. Remand status of the offender and the nature of the court and the proceedings under which it was operating (summary or solemn (indictment));
3. Criminal history of the offender;
4. Previous sentencing history, if any;
5. Social workers' assessments of the risk of custody;
6. SER recommendation as to sentence;
7. Final court outcome.

The number of cases (SERs) involved in the current study was: Muirville (251) (one phase only); Cambusneal (645); Duncansburgh (837); Rutherton (180).

In each site, research staff were involved in various committees, project groups and working parties associated with the development and subsequent operation of the project or initiative involved. This involvement included relevant meetings with sheriffs where these took place.

The four probation initiatives

The four research sites are described briefly below, with relevant details concerning each probation project and key features of the research involvement. By agreement with the authorities concerned, all identifying information was removed from the research reports and the following names of research sites and their authorities are, therefore, fictionalised.

The Muirville Groupwork Project

The Muirville Groupwork Project, located in a deprived inner-city area within Western Region, was established to provide a service to three of the District's area teams as an alternative to custody groupwork programme for young adult offenders (16 - 21.) Participants are normally subject to probation orders with a condition of attendance and the project serves mainly one Sheriff Court. The project began life as an Urban Aid-funded community scheme undertaking preventative work with young offenders and others considered at risk. Later, a multi-functional approach was developed to include specialised probation facilities as a direct alternative to custody; an after-care facility; and a drop-in facility.   Referrals were taken from two local area teams in cases either remanded in custody or where assessment for community service was requested by the court.

Continuing low numbers in the early stages led to decisions to widen the catchment area and to improve referral systems. Once research involvement had been initiated, however, it was agreed to focus only on those cases which fell within the higher tariff category. In many ways, the history of the project and the continuation in post of existing staff made it difficult to achieve the radical shift in direction envisaged by the authorities when the project moved to mainstream social work funding. The preventative youth-work ethos which had prevailed for many years made it particularly difficult to develop and maintain a strict alternative to custody orientation.

The Cambusneal Probation Initiative

Cambusneal City is one of five divisions in Northern Region. The probation initiative involved working collaboratively with the three adult care teams covering Cambusneal City and with the Community Service team covering the city and two other divisions. The city has a population of approximately 200,000 and has eleven areas designated as Areas of Priority Treatment. Cambusneal Sheriff Court covers Cambusneal City and an adjoining Division. Social work teams were organised along 'almost specialised' lines, with staff being allowed to take up to 15per cent work outside their own specialism.

Northern Region originally became involved in the research in order to help clarify and develop probation practice within the Cambusneal City adult care teams. Discussions at management level were followed by a number of training days which took place outwith the normal work-place and involved team members and research staff. Attendance was obligatory and the purpose of these sessions was to encourage social work staff to pose fundamental questions about the nature of probation. It became increasingly apparent that the probation assessment process and SER practice were highly subjective and individualised. This came as little surprise to the researchers who had reported on such matters at an earlier stage of the research (Williams and Creamer, 1987.)

General agreement was reached to work towards differential probation practice targeted at clients at different levels of the sentencing tariff and with varying social work needs. A special meeting with the Cambusneal sheriffs was initiated to begin a consultative process which continued throughout the life of the research. In the main, the sheriffs welcomed the new initiative whilst reserving the right to view each case on its own merits. Working groups were set up to develop appropriate standards for each of the proposed probation regimes - 'needs-orientated' ('type A'); 'offence-orientated' ('type B'); and 'criminal justice orientated' with a specific condition of unpaid work ('type C'.) Attention was also given to the introduction of a ten week period of deferred sentence to be used for in-depth assessment of suitability for probation. A series of draft standards papers was produced, together with information leaflets aimed at different groups (clients, social workers, court personnel etc.) Final proposals were discussed and agreed at another meeting with sheriffs. Letters were then sent out to defence agents, procurators fiscal and clerks of court outlining the new initiative.

The Duncansburgh Community Probation Project

The Community Probation Project, located within a division of Western Region, was established to provide a service to Duncansburgh Sheriff Court and to the five social work area teams within the District. The target group was that of young adult offenders (16 - 25) considered to be at serious risk of custody. All participants are subjects of a probation order with a condition of attendance at the project. The area served by the project contains mixed housing stock although there are a number of designated Areas of Priority Treatment. The history of the Duncansburgh project was not dissimilar to that of the Muirville Groupwork Project (above) in that both had started life as local community resources for young offenders or young people at risk, initially funded by Urban-Aid. Both projects underwent a radical change when taken into mainstream social work funding to offer a high tariff alternative to custody. The processes by which this transition was achieved by the two projects, however, differed significantly.

In Duncansburgh, the opportunity was taken when the team leader post became vacant to appoint a senior social worker with very specific plans for an alternatives to custody project. Basic research on SERs was conducted at Duncansburgh Sheriff Court; the premises were completely refurbished; a widespread consultation process initiated; and proposals for the new unit were finalised and presented to the area teams. During this period, specialist groupwork staff were recruited and a successful meeting with sheriffs was arranged at which the proposals were presented. Thus an important change of culture and emphasis was achieved, reinforced by a change in the project name. The researchers became involved once this shift had been achieved.

The Rutherton Alternative to Detention Project

The Rutherton Alternative to Detention Project was sponsored and managed by a large national voluntary organisation but funded mainly by central government, through the Urban Programme, and by Western Regional Council. The catchment area for the project was co-terminous with the area served by the five social work area teams and included two district burghs with characteristic inner city problems. Unemployment and poverty rates were high (30 per cent in one burgh living at or below Income Support level.) Rutherton district also includes rural and semi-rural tracts showing similar problems of poverty and unemployment. Within the Sheriffdom there are five Areas of Priority Treatment.

Early discussions took place within one of the area teams about developing probation into a more credible community alternative for the court. These resulted in a seminar attended by a wide range of participants, including local sheriffs, at which it was agreed that it should be a priority to develop better community-based provision for higher tariff offenders. Fortuitously, a representative of the voluntary agency approached Western Region shortly afterwards with a proposal to set up a demonstration alternative to detention project within the region. After discussion with senior managers, agreement was reached to establish such a project within the Sheriffdom of Rutherton. The project was to include elements of groupwork, intensive supervision and counselling, focusing on up to thirty young adult offenders (16-20) per year, and was established with an emphasis on public education and the widespread dissemination of information to the courts and others.

The researchers became involved at an early stage and advised on the conduct of a research survey commissioned by the voluntary agency to identify the type of young offender most commonly sentenced to custody at Rutherton Sheriff Court. The Project Leader was someone with considerable experience of running similar schemes elsewhere. Despite this, and the agreement and support of the local courts, a number of difficulties were experienced in relation to staff recruitment, relationships with the statutory authority, the inevitable pressure to be seen to succeed and divergent agendas among the many sectors represented within the project management group.

Methodological issues

Since the main aim of the study was to explore how effective the probation projects were in diverting serious offenders from custody, it was considered essential to develop a reliable standard indicator which could be used by SER authors and researchers alike to assess the level of risk that a court might impose a custodial sentence in a particular case. This measure needed to be reliable over time to permit longitudinal comparisons within each research site and, more importantly, 'transportable' enough to permit cross-site comparisons to be made. The latter function is, of course, seriously complicated by the well-known variations in sentencing patterns between courts which make risk of custody a relative concept dependent on 'local' variables. By contrast, it may be assumed that the seriousness of a case might be assessed on a more universal basis by considering factors such as the nature of the offences, the previous criminal and sentencing history of the offender and so on.

After experimenting with the Cambridgeshire Risk of Custody Scale and discussions with its author David Bale, this was found to be unsuitable for the Scottish context and it was decided to develop a new scale *ab initio*. One of the requirements agreed with the research funding body was that the scale developed should be straightforward enough to permit its use within mainstream SER practice. The researchers were also keen to utilise data that was readily available to SER authors and which required the minimum of interpretation (i.e. so-called 'hard' data.) In the event the factors which emerged as variables in what has become known as *'the DUNSCORE methodology'* (University of Dundee Risk of Custody Score) are all readily available to social workers early in the SER compilation process. The method by which the scale was developed has been described elsewhere (Creamer, Hartley and Williams, 1992a; Creamer, Ennis and Williams 1994) but essentially it consisted of testing a wide range of variables (offender biography, current and previous offence and sentencing factors and SER variables) for statistical correlation with known custodial outcomes. The strongest correlated factors were retained then weighted experimentally until a satisfactory relationship was obtained between the DUNSCORE and the likelihood of a custodial sentence. Each case can then be given a score which expresses the level of risk of custody.

A major advantage of such an instrument is that it is possible to make comparisons between sites where the sentencing patterns are different. The first step in achieving this is to divide samples into *risk categories*, based on the percentage of cases in that category which receive custodial sentences (the researchers most regularly use a categorisation based on low, medium, serious and very serious risk bands.) It is then possible to explore within each location how the DUNSCORE relates to risk of custody, *within the local sentencing context*. A comparison between two of the research sites will help to illustrate this technique.

Table 6.1
Relationship between DUNSCORE and risk of custody by area

	Rutherton			Muirville	
DUNSCORE	% custody	Risk category	DUNSCORE	% custody	Risk category
0-3	9.2	Low	0-2	14.5	Low
4	23.1	Medium	3-4	32.4	Serious
5	38.9	Serious	5+	59.2	V. Serious
6+	82.6	V. Serious			

It can be seen that in the Rutherton court, the risk of custody does not become serious until a DUNSCORE of 5 is reached, whereas in Muirville a DUNSCORE as low as 3 could indicate this same level of risk. This has to do with the different sentencing patterns of the two courts and had important implications for the projects in terms of which offenders they ought to be targeting in order to ensure that they were not inappropriately referred. Given the variations in demography and geography between the research areas, it came as something of a surprise to discover that the percentage of serious cases dealt with by the respective courts did not differ significantly (per cent of cases with DUNSCORE of 5+ Muirville 27 per cent; Cambusneal 24 per cent; Duncansburgh 26 per cent; Rutherton 29 per cent.) This makes the differences in custodial sentencing rates between the sites more striking (Muirville 29 per cent; Cambusneal 20 per cent; Duncansburgh 31 per cent; Rutherton 26 per cent.) To simplify the analysis a dichotomy between *higher tariff* (serious and very serious risk) and *lower tariff* (low and medium risk) was used and this terminology is employed later in describing the results of the study.

In order to allow for the possibility that, over time, the samples of SERs used for monitoring would contain different proportions of the more serious cases (thus making straightforward longitudinal comparisons invalid), the researchers used the baseline data obtained in each of the four retrospective studies as a basis for comparison but corrected for changes in the proportion of serious cases appearing in the later samples. This was done by taking the percentage of custodial outcomes appearing within each risk category in the retrospective sample and using these to extrapolate from the current data, adjusted for the different risk band make-up of the sample, to predict an *anticipated custodial outcome* from the sample, i.e. the numbers of custodial sentences which might, all other things being equal, have resulted. This gave a measure of the 'value added' introduced by the projects once they became operational.

Following stimulating discussions with Don McLeod a probation officer in Macclesfield about the development of team monitoring strategies, the researchers borrowed two concepts which have proved to be of considerable serviceability. These are the notions of *'diversion rate'* (the percentage of *higher tariff* cases *not* receiving a custodial sentence) and *'error rate'* (the percentage of *lower tariff* cases actually *sentenced to custody*) (Creamer, Ennis and Williams, 1994.) These are used in what follows.

Results of the study

Distribution of cases within risk bands

In Cambusneal, the proportion of cases falling into the *higher tariff* category *increased* gradually but consistently over the research period (13.2 per cent to 25.3 per cent), suggesting an increased preparedness by the court to request SERs in the more serious cases and therefore to consider community disposals. This was not the case in any of the other sites where the proportion of higher tariff cases on which SERs were requested *decreased* (Muirville and Duncansburgh 39 per cent to 34 per cent; Rutherton 29 per cent to 18 per cent.) The higher proportion of *higher tariff* cases in Muirville and Duncansburgh (the first figure in each case represents the baseline data obtained from the retrospective study) reflects the high custodial sentencing rate in these sites and the lower point on the DUNSCORE at which offenders faced a serious risk of custody.

Anticipated custodial outcomes

Had the *custodial rates* which had pertained in the retrospective study for all sites been maintained, then a larger number of custodial disposals could emerged. Comparing the anticipated numbers with the actual numbers yields the following pattern:

Table 6.2
Expected and actual custodial disposals

Site	Expected no.	Actual no.
Muirville	63	54
Cambusneal	153	102
Duncansburgh	241	158
Rutherton	37	10

In all sites, therefore, the custodial rates (in SER cases) *fell* significantly during the research period (Muirville 29 per cent to 22 per cent; Cambusneal 20 per cent to 16 per cent; Duncansburgh 31 per cent to 18 per cent; Rutherton 26 per cent to 6 per cent.) The change was most noticeable for the second phase of the study, suggesting an improvement in targeting strategies within the probation schemes. Follow-up studies in one of the sites show that this trend has been maintained with a small increase in custodial sentencing rates over a two-year period but no return to baseline rates established in the retrospective study (Williams and Creamer, 1993.)

Diversion from custody

The most dramatic proportionate decreases in custodial sentencing were in Duncansburgh and Rutherton and in both cases this was due in no small part to a noticeable *reduction* in the number of lower tariff cases receiving custodial sentences (the *'error rate'*) (Duncansburgh 16 per cent to 6 per cent; Rutherton 11 per cent to 2 per cent; Muirville 15 per cent to 12 per cent.) In Cambusneal the 'error' rate remained constant at around 10 per cent throughout the whole research period.

At all four sites the proportion of higher tariff cases *not* receiving custody (the *'diversion rate'*) *went up* significantly during the research period, in one case quite dramatically (Rutherton 37 per cent to 78 per cent; Duncansburgh 47 per cent to 62 per cent; Cambusneal 50 per cent to 67 per cent; Muirville 50 per cent to 59 per cent.) This suggested strongly that the projects were demonstrating the intended impact on overall rates of custodial sentencing. In Cambusneal this greater 'diversion' was achieved significantly within the *very serious* risk band, where only about half the anticipated number of cases received custodial sentences, suggesting a very effective targeting of the type C probation order.

Court use of non-custodial disposals

These higher diversion rates from custody were associated with different patterns in the use of community disposals (standard and intensive probation; community service) within the four research sites. In Muirville, for example, there was a *small increase* in the overall use of community disposals in the higher tariff category (25 per cent to 29 per cent). At the same time, however, the groupwork project itself accounted for a *reducing* proportion of these cases over the research period (8 per cent to 4 per cent.) and a corresponding increase in its use for *lower-tariff* offenders (2 per cent to 6 per cent), strongly suggesting the dangers of 'tariff escalation'.

In Duncansburgh the pattern of use of the community disposals was more complicated in that it *increased sharply* in phase 1 (22 per cent to 45 per cent) only to *fall* again in phase two (45 per cent to 30 per cent), suggesting an unusually large 'experimental' effect in the former period. These patterns reflected fairly accurately underlying changes in the use of community disposals in *lower tariff* cases. The large increase in phase 1 appeared to be due to a significant but *unsustained* use of the special probation project. The researchers were left to conclude that the reduction in custodial sentencing could not be attributed directly to an increase in the use of community alternatives involving social work and this created concerns about the effectiveness of the 'gate-keeping' for the Community Probation Project.

Within the Rutherton site, there was a *dramatic increase* in the use of community disposals in higher tariff cases (10 per cent to 47 per cent), a factor which was clearly associated with the reduction in custody. The availability of the Alternative to Detention Project accounted in part for this phenomenon but there were also noticeable increases in the use of standard probation and community service in higher tariff cases. A *similar increase* was found in Cambusneal (26 per cent to 47 per cent) with the biggest increase occurring in phase 2, an encouraging sign from the point of view of sustainability. The use of intensive (type C) probation was one factor, but there was also a noticeable shift in the use of community service towards the higher tariff cases (10 per cent to 28 per cent).

The researchers were interested to explore by what means the above changes in the patterns of sentencing had come about and, in particular, the part played by SER writers through their sentencing recommendations. Once again, each site showed particular characteristics which are described below.

In Cambusneal, the rate of recommendations for probation *reduced* overall, although such recommendations became *more focused* on higher tariff cases. The acceptance rate by the court *increased* over the research period, especially in the higher tariff cases. Only rarely did the court make a probation order without a clear recommendation for this within the SER, although this was not true of community service orders where the courts showed more independence of action.The same pattern was found for community service recommendations and disposals so that the number of orders of both types increased significantly in higher tariff cases. The most noticeable feature was the overall increase in the acceptance rate of recommendations in higher tariff cases (36 per cent to 67 per cent (phase 2)), suggesting an enhanced credibility over time.

At the Rutherton site the *slight drop* in recommendations for community disposals was more than compensated for by a *dramatic increase* in the acceptance rate by the court (standard probation 44 per cent to 77 per cent; community service 15 per cent to 86 per cent), a feature in both low and high tariff cases. Only one in 17 of recommendations for the project was *not* accepted by the court, resulting in a high 'conversion rate' and highlighting the importance of having an agreed policy in relation to the appropriateness of such recommendations. As in Cambusneal, this factor was considered to demonstrate an improved credibility for social workers within the court setting.

In Duncansburgh, as elsewhere, there was no evidence that the introduction of the probation project had the effect of moving other 'social work' disposals lower in the tariff and the overall rate of recommendations for standard probation in higher tariff cases *increased slightly* during the research period. The acceptance rate for these, however, after showing a *sharp increase* in phase 1, *dropped to baseline levels* again in phase 2, suggesting perhaps that no significant change in court practice had been brought about. In respect of the special probation project, there was considerable fluctuation over the course of the research both in terms of SER recommendation practice and in the responses from the court. The court in phase 1 rarely imposed this disposal without a clear positive recommendation in favour of it and, in the vast majority of cases, sentenced to custody those for whom there was no such recommendation. This suggested that the court had started out with a clear view of the project as a strict alternative to custody and also emphasised the crucial nature of the social workers' role in gate-keeping. In phase 2, however, the court showed more independence of action, making a number of project orders in the absence of recommendation and using other non-custodial disposals for those not considered suitable. The recommendation rates for community disposals in higher tariff cases in Duncansburgh were consistently *higher than average* even in the retrospective study and this indicated a *proactive* stance on the part of SER authors (Williams and Creamer, 1988.) If there was, therefore, a problem it was in the interface between social workers and the court, especially in the later phases of the research.

As has already been indicated, the use of the probation project in Muirville moved more towards the *lower tariff* cases as the research progressed and this was in part the result of an increase in the number of recommendations in such cases. The court's rate of acceptance for higher tariff project recommendations also fell, suggesting a *loss of credibility* in at least some cases. There was an overall *increase* in the use of probation; in *higher tariff* cases resulting from an increased number of accepted recommendations and in *lower tariff* cases resulting from the courts imposing orders without these being recommended. It was difficult, therefore, to discern a clear strategy, agreed between social workers and the courts, in respect of the most appropriate use of probation. With the inception of the project, the number of higher tariff recommendations for community service *decreased* and the court tended to make more 'independent' CS orders in lower tariff cases.

Discussion and conclusions

The results summarised above indicate clearly that, despite the four experimental probation schemes having a common objective (i.e. that of decreasing the number of custodial sentences by means of increasing the number of community disposals in serious cases) this was pursued in different ways with different results. Given the historic sentencing patterns of different courts and the presuppositions and preferred practices of SER authors, it is immediately apparent that even such a simple objective needs to be pursued with this 'local' context fully in mind. Furthermore, in evaluating such initiatives, it is not enough simply to look at the numbers of cases falling into the various disposal categories since this practice masks both the subtleties of outcome and, more importantly, the unforeseen consequences. To explore these, some common objective measure is needed whereby the 'profile' of offenders given the various sentences can be monitored across sites and over time. Without such a measure, the introduction of a project intended to divert serious offenders from custody could easily have a deleterious, and undetected, effect on other community disposals (e.g. moving the use of community service lower in the tariff as in Muirville.)

At the simplest level, it can be said that each of the schemes was successful in that an *overall reduction was achieved in the custodial sentencing rate* (of SER cases) during the research period and the probation projects were demonstrated to have contributed to this achievement. With the exception of Muirville, the reduction in custodial disposals was remarkable. In Duncansburgh and Rutherton not only was the 'diversion' rate increased, but the 'error' rate was also significantly reduced. This latter achievement was in itself commendable in that it reflected a much lower percentage of lower tariff cases resulting in custody. In Cambusneal where there was a substantial increase in the *number* of higher tariff cases under consideration, the overall custodial *rate* was still reduced, demonstrating a real reduction in custodial sentences for more serious offenders. In this site we also noted an increasing preparedness by sentencers to request SERs in the *very serious* risk of custody category, also suggesting an increased willingness on their part to consider community disposals in such cases.

Analysis of the retrospective samples revealed quite different court sentencing practices in respect of the use of custody. Because of this, the determination of appropriate risk categories for the four research sites (i.e. identifying the point on the DUNSCORE at which risk of custody became serious) became an essential starting point for evaluation. These variations strongly suggested that offenders in Muirville and Duncansburgh were much more likely to receive a custodial sentence than their counterparts (with similar criminal histories and committing similar offences) appearing before courts in Cambusneal and Rutherton. Detailed studies revealed that offenders appearing before the former courts for relatively minor offences (i.e. those with gravity scores of 1 or 2) without having received a recent probation or community service order did *actually* receive custodial sentences more frequently than was the case in the latter courts. This helped to confirm the reliability of the DUNSCORE in its predictive role. The only possible explanation available was that in these courts there was a prevalent, if somewhat dubious, belief that a custodial sentence imposed sufficiently early in the career of an offender was justified in that it would have a deterrent effect on future behaviour.

As has been observed, the actual attainment of decreasing custodial sentencing was reached by different routes. In Cambusneal and Rutherton, for example, the increase in court acceptance rates for social work recommendations improved dramatically, and not only for the special probation projects. Acceptance rates for standard probation and community service also increased substantially. Indeed, in Cambusneal, it was the increase in recommendations and acceptance rates for community service which was demonstrated to have played a significant role in the increased diversion rate. This was an unintended but welcome spin-off, resulting from a much clearer targeting of community service resources towards higher tariff cases. In Rutherton, where the acceptance rate for the project was particularly high, this too was accompanied by an increase in the acceptance rates for standard probation and community service. It was concluded that in these two sites in particular there had been a growing confidence on the part of the court in social workers' assessment of suitability for these disposals, accompanied by an *increasing overall confidence* in the appropriateness of statutory community supervision in the more serious cases.

In Duncansburgh, it seemed likely that the shift in court practice with respect to the probation project in phase 2 indicated a growing reluctance to rely on the exclusive gate-keeping role of the social workers. Interestingly, this change in court response to social work recommendations was not, as might have been expected, accompanied by an increase in the custodial rate. On the contrary, the custodial disposal rate was reduced even further over this second period.

Only in Muirville, was the alternative to custody project in operation at the start of our data collection. Thus the changes in practice within that site may be a clearer indication of what can take place once initiatives of this kind have become established. The shift which took place in the use of the project increasingly for lower tariff cases was clearly related not only to the low *acceptance* rate of higher tariff recommendations for the project but also to a reduction in the project *recommendation* rate in these more serious cases. The Muirville situation, inter alia, convinced the researchers of the need for continuous monitoring of this type of alternative to custody scheme. Lessons from the past (in particular the increasing use of community service in lower tariff cases) should caution against the assumption that the existence of gate-keeping criteria alone will guarantee continuing accuracy of project targeting, however well publicised this information may be.

The use of the DUNSCORE and other standard measures of risk of custody and seriousness of case has an important role to play in the monitoring and evaluation of projects of this kind. As assessment tools they can alert social workers to the degree of risk of custody facing each subject of an SER and can thereby act as a check on the appropriateness of sentencing recommendations. We would encourage the idea that recommendations for community service, standard probation and particularly alternative to custody initiatives be restricted largely to cases which reach the point on the DUNSCORE at which risk of custody becomes *serious*, unless extenuating circumstances can be clearly demonstrated. Without this strict attention to gate-keeping, a drift downwards in the tariff appears very likely.

At the conclusion of our evaluation of the four initiatives we were conscious of the fact that three (if not four) of them had achieved a much wider success than perhaps was either anticipated or that the small scale and throughput of the projects could justify. In claiming, as we have, that in none of the sites could the probation initiatives themslves be demonstrated to have been responsible *exclusively* for the reduction in custody achieved, we have not intended to underestimate the valuable contribution which they have obviously made. Rather, it is to say that by addressing seriously the problem of inappropriate custodial sentencing and attempting to increase the range of community disposals available to the courts, the impact such schemes have made has been wider reaching.

Thus in at least three of the research sites what we have called an *'alternative to custody ethos'* has been established. This has been brought about by a combination of factors such as a heightened awareness among social workers of the importance of a careful consideration of community disposals in higher tariff cases and a willingness to recommend these to the courts; an increased confidence among sentencers in the appropriateness of SER recommendations and a greater willingness to use non-custodial disposals in serious cases; together with better communication between the two groups, resulting in greater clarity of expectation. The detailed discussions and negotiations with sentencers which were involved in establishing the experimental projects tended to produce this ethos as a crucial by-product. If it can be sustained in these locations, and introduced elsewhere, there is good reason to believe that the sort of results reported in this study can be reproduced elsewhere and can become mainstream practice over time. Our own follow-up studies indicate that this may already be the case in at least one site (Williams and Creamer, 1993.)

Note

1. Throughout the text the term 'rate' is used to express as a measure the proportion of cases in a particular group or category which demonstrate some other property or characteristic. Thus the *custody rate* is the percentage of cases of a particular kind which receive custodial sentences. Similarly, the *recommendation rate* is the proportion of SER cases of a specific kind (e.g. higher tariff) which receive a particular sentencing recommendation. The whole study is SER based and so overall custody and other rates refer only to such cases (i.e. the figures in this category do not correspond with the total number of custodial or other sentences passed by the courts concerned).

References

Creamer, A., Hartley, L. and Williams, B. (1992a), *The Probation Alternative: A Study of the Impact of Four Enhanced Probation Schemes on Sentencing*, Scottish Office Central Research Unit, Edinburgh.

Creamer, A., Hartley, L. and Williams, B. (1992b), *The Probation Alternative: Case Studies in the Establishment of Alternative to Custody Schemes in Scotland*, Scottish Office Central Research Unit , Edinburgh.

Creamer, A., Ennis, E. and Williams, B. (1994), *The Dunscore: a social enquiry practice and evaluation tool for social workers and social work managers in Scotland*, Scottish Office and University of Dundee, Dundee.

Ford, R., Ditton, J. and Laybourn, A. (1992), *Probation in Scotland: Process and Practice*, Scottish Office Central Research Unit, Edinburgh.

Williams, B. and Creamer, A., (1987), *Social Enquiry in a Changing Context*, Scottish Office Central Research Unit, Edinburgh.

Williams, B., Creamer, A. and Hartley, L. (1988), *The Second Chance: Scottish Probation Orders in the Late 1980s* (first and second reports), Unpublished research reports to the Social Work Services Group of the Scottish Office.

Williams, B., Creamer, A. and Hartley, L., (1990), 'Probation as an Alternative to Custody', in M Adler, and A Miller, (eds.), *Socio-Legal Research in the Scottish Courts* (vol.2), Scottish Office Central Research Unit, Edinburgh.

Williams, B. and Creamer, A., (1993), *The Targeting and Monitoring of Community-based Sanctions: A Follow-up Case Study*, unpublished paper given to the British Criminology Conference, Cardiff.

ACKNOWLEDGEMENTS

The research was funded by a grant from the Social Work Services Group at the Scottish Office. We wish to acknowledge with gratitude the invaluable assistance of our research colleague Linda Hartley who worked on the project with us. Thanks are also due to David Bale, Catherine Fitzmaurice and Don McLeod.

7 Trying to unravel the Gordian Knot: an evaluation of community service orders

Jean Hine

Understanding the context

Confusion of Purpose

The complexities and confusions about community service and its role and underlying philosophy are long standing and well documented (e.g. Young 1979; Pease and McWilliams, 1980; Pease, 1983; Wright, 1984). None of this is surprising, however, given the multi-faceted nature of community service, present in the initial proposal for its introduction (Home Office, 1971). Sentencers could view the disposal in a wide variety of guises - punishment, reparation, a constructive means of filling idle time, etc.

Pease and McWilliams (1980) suggested four possible (though extreme) ideal typical alternative futures for community service which might emerge from the then current diversity (p.138):

1. *Bureaucratisation* (emphasis on getting the work done, no probation officers involved),
2. *Probationisation* (emphasis by probation officers on caring aspects of CS, rampant discretion),
3. *Penalisation* (move towards 'tougher' work and impersonal environment, enforcement crisis) and
4. *Standardisation* (national agreement about the role of community service and administrative rules for its operation).

This latter 'cameo' was their preferred option, and they hoped it would arise out of informed debate within the probation service. They argued against giving community service 'a period of benign neglect' (p viii), predicting:

96

Benign neglect would mean that community service would become ossified in its present forms or in forms in which it is shaped by pragmatic decision and economic circumstances. The longer the delay and the larger and more varied the scheme, the less possible it will become to achieve purposive change. (p.viii)

When our research was commissioned by the Home Office in 1987, there had been a long period of 'benign neglect' for community service, one which was about to end abruptly with the introduction of draft National Standards for Community Service in 1988. Whilst ACOP had worked on the 'standardisation' model and introduced national guidelines (ACOP 1983), these were voluntary and not taken up by all probation areas. Indeed, one of the reasons for the Home Office commissioning Birmingham University to undertake the national study was to examine the range of schemes which existed in practice at the time; a range which covered almost every conceivable mix of bureaucratisation, probationisation and penalisation. The Home Office decided however, as part of its new penal strategy, that consistency and known standards were required to increase sentencers' confidence in the community service order, introducing the standards formally (Home Office, 1989) with a requirement that all probation areas implement them. National Standards were also introduced in Scotland at about the same time, but they took a different focus, so that 'community service in Scotland has retained a more rehabilitative, offender-centred orientation than in England & Wales' (Smith, 1996).

The late 1980s were a time of hopeful uncertainty for the Probation Service. The Green Paper 'Punishment, Custody and the Community' (Home Office, 1988) contained proposals for reducing the use of custodial sentences. The paper proposed increased use of community sentences, but this required a 'toughening' of existing community sentences and the introduction of a new disposal - the combination order. Whilst the proposals assured a future for the probation service (something which had been in doubt) they required continued change in emphasis for the service towards providing 'punishment in the community' (a move in the direction of 'penalisation' in Pease and McWilliams' terms) rather than help for the offender. This has been described by Rutherford (1993) as a time of 'penal parsimony' in policy terms, but this policy required fundamental shift in the way in which the Probation Service was viewed from outside. David Faulkner (1989) described this required shift:

... transformation from a social work agency to a criminal justice service with a social work base must be completed if the service is to do what is now expected of it, especially in the context of the

Green Paper ... important for the service to demonstrate its credibility and commitment to dealing with the crime problem, and not to undermine its credibility with too much abstract argument about care and control, or about the nature of punishment. (p.607)

Complexity of Task

The need for balance in managing community service had been commented upon soon after its introduction, by Jenny West (1976)

... basic problems about the relationship between the offender, the courts, the probation service and the community ... the community service organiser must have the capacity to sit on a number of diverging fences. (p.69)

Ten years later, the complexity of the task of managing and running community service was amply demonstrated in a survey of probation areas undertaken for the Community Service Committee of the Association of Chief Officers of Probation in 1985. The authors (Adair et al., 1987) reported:

...Community Service in the mid-1980s is not a straightforward concept, but more a system or constellation of balancing tensions which need to be managed. These include the key components such as its organisational structure, staffing, types of placements used, its position in the tariff, and so on." (p.2)

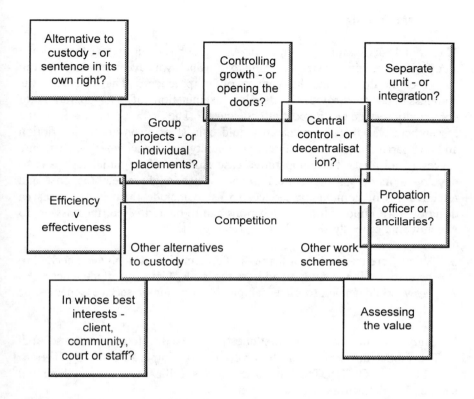

Figure 7.1: The complexities of managing community service

The above chart is reproduced from the interim report of that survey (Adair et al.,1987, Appendix 1). It summarises the overwhelming impression conveyed by the respondents to this questionnaire of the complexities of managing community service and delivering a service with such a wide range of competing demands. This chart illustrates the main internal management issues in relation to community service at the time. It hints at the wide range of stakeholders who have expectations of community service and what it should achieve. It illuminates the problems faced by the research team when it began its work in 1988. The brief provided by the Home Office was broad: to provide a detailed evaluation of the operation of community service. It allowed considerable scope for determining the detail of the work around core requirements for (a) an assessment of cost and its relationship to outcomes of orders and (b) a substantial quantitative element identifying features related to the successful outcome of community service.

The research design

This complexity/confusion formed the background for designing the national study of community service - a complexity which was eventually mirrored in the research design and its application in practice. The research was commissioned to provide a detailed examination of the operation of community service and its cost effectiveness. The first decision made by the researchers was that the research would consist of an in-depth description and comparison of several different community service schemes rather than a survey of all areas, i.e. comparative case studies. The initial task was to develop a model of the critical factors which might affect the cost and effectiveness of community service, so as to include them in the research design. Two important initial questions had to be addressed, the answers to which would crucially shape the research project:

1. What were the important features of community service which needed to be assessed in the study to address the issue of success/effectiveness?
2. How could an appropriate sample of community service schemes be chosen?

In reality, consideration of the first question enabled us to answer the second.

The model developed was basically a very simple one of INPUTS -> PROCESS -> OUTPUTS, but its detailed specification was anything but simple. We defined these concepts very broadly.

INPUTS   included not just the offender subject to community service, but also all factors which affected the general nature of the scheme. The researchers realised that this was actually the most critical element of the description: we posited that many of the inputs would have a significant effect on the nature of the process and experience of community service for the offenders, and ultimately the outputs. It was important therefore that schemes be included in the research which represented a range of different features. Some of the information about 'inputs' was readily available either from published sources or from the previous survey by the ACOP Community Service Committee (Adair et al., 1987), but little was readily available about process and outputs. This led us to the view that the available information about inputs should be used to choose the sample of schemes for study, and that the main focus of the study would be on describing process and output aspects of the model.

PROCESS   had to be described in detail, rather than viewed as a 'black box'. In what ways did the inputs shape the process of the order, and interact to produce the outputs?

OUTPUTS   are the effectiveness measures of community service and would be affected by the 'inputs' and the way in which the offenders were 'processed'. It took account of the wide range of stakeholders in community service and tried to reflect their expectations. Figure 7.2 shows the main stakeholders who have an interest in community service and its success. The diagram is neat and well balanced implying all stakeholders having an equal impact on the shape which community service takes. In reality there are continuing shifts in this balance, so the picture changes over time. Nor will the pattern be the same in each Probation Area, or even necessarily in each scheme within an area: local circumstances, interest groups and the extent of their interest and influence will determine the local picture. All pictures however will show greater influence and pull from the four stakeholders towards the top of the diagram (practitioners, local management, Home Office and sentencers), than from the bottom (beneficiaries, public, offenders).

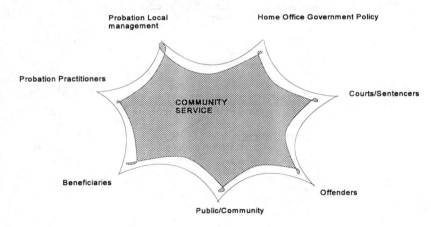

Figure 7.2: Stakeholders in community service

The factors which we included under each of these headings is shown in Figure 7.3.

INPUTS

Geography, *eg urban/rural*
Local sentencing practices, *eg types of offence*
Numbers and lengths of orders
Characteristics of offenders given CS, *ie criminal history, skills, attitudes, age, gender, race, employment*
National and local policies, *eg alternative to custody, pre-sentence assessment*
Local management structure, style and systems
Staffing patterns, *eg numbers, type, grade*
Equipment and resources available, *eg buildings, workshops, minibus*
Available work, *ie amount, type, location, agency availability*

PROCESS

Assessment of CS workers
Assessment and organisation of work
Allocating workers to tasks
Supervision of workers
Enforcing rules about attendance and performance
Tracking worker progress, crediting hours worked
Responding to breaches of rules
Maintaining records
Allocating resources
Reviewing scheme operation and performance
Planning and controlling expenditure

OUTPUTS

Completed orders
Orders not completed
Value of work done
Effect upon worker attitudes
Smooth running and consistent operation of scheme
Staff morale

Figure 7.3: A model for evaluating community service effectiveness

Choosing the schemes

The nature of variation within community service schemes means that no two probation areas are identical: indeed, there is often variation within probation areas. This meant that it would not be possible to choose a sample which could be said to be 'representative' of all community service schemes. In fact it would not have been helpful to the aims of the study to choose a few 'representative' schemes. The study was particularly concerned to look for differences between schemes and to try and assess whether these differences had a differential impact on outcome. This meant that a sample of schemes was required which were as different as possible from one another, highlighting the key features of debate and controversy. The task for the researchers would be to attempt to isolate these features to determine their effect.

The choice of probation areas to be studied in the research was determined by two priorities. Firstly, a need to be able to study a wide range of schemes so as to be able to shed as much light as possible on the features highlighted in our conceptual model of community service. Secondly, practical consideration required that the schemes studied were reasonably accessible to the researchers, minimising travel so far as possible. The first decision was to determine the number of schemes to be studied. In the light of the depth of study which would be required we decided that a maximum of six schemes would be feasible.

Information and published data about community service were available on a Probation Service basis only, and thus for the first stage of the sampling complete probation services were chosen. Following detailed discussion and negotiation with managers in the chosen probation areas a more precise definition of 'scheme' within the area was determined and a decision made about the exact coverage of the research within the area. Six probation areas were initially approached: five welcomed participation in the study, but one felt it would not be convenient at the time. A substitute area was chosen and some pilot work undertaken, but that area too felt unable to participate. At that point it was agreed that the five areas which had initially agreed provided sufficient variety to enable a valid comparative study to be undertaken.

The final five areas studied in the research were indeed very different:

Area A: Small county area, mainly rural, relatively affluent. CS sentence in own right with high repeat use. High proportion probation managed caring projects and clubs.

Area B: Large county, dispersed with some urban centres and some high levels deprivation. High proportion previous custody for those given CS. No probation officer staff below Assistant Chief Probation Officer. Use of agency placements for community involvement and economy. The scheme had a leaning towards the 'bureaucratisation' model.

Area C: Compact urban centre in large metropolitan service, generally affluent but recent recession. High use CS, especially short orders, and low use probation. Quick throughput and strict enforcement policy. This scheme had a leaning towards the 'penalisation' model.

Area D: Central conurbation of large metropolitan service with high unemployment and deprivation. Complex, functionally supervised superstructure with very varied work range.

Area E: Dispersed rural county with some urban areas and mixed unemployment. Use of volunteer supervisors. Strong emphasis on agency placements and absence of industrialised projects. This scheme leant towards the 'probationisation' model.

The research methods

The complexity of community service and the wide range of features which we were attempting to study resulted in a research design which incorporated a considerable variety of research methods, both qualitative and quantitative. The wide possible scope of the exercise required decisions about what to leave out, the main component of which was sentencers views. A similar study of community service in Scotland (McIvor, 1992) required a similar range of methods, but being undertaken over a series of smaller studies rather than one large one was able to include more aspects. Our research methods are described briefly below.

Analysis of Policy Documents:

Each scheme was asked to provide us with their important papers which would enable us to develop a picture of the local policy, aims, objectives and organisation of their community service scheme. These documents took a variety of forms, including official policy and committee papers, minutes of meetings, leaflets for sentencers, staff and offenders and reports and evaluations of schemes.

Observation:

A key feature of this research was the amount of time spent on site with community service managers, staff and workers. Some of this was structured, for instance the examination of a sample of projects in each area, but much was informal and unstructured and occurred whilst other formal work was being undertaken. This enabled the researchers to collect a lot of supplementary information about the way in which schemes worked. Observations were made of team meetings, work projects, court hearings.

Interviews:

Formal structured interviews were carried out with a range of informants. Whilst wide ranging and detailed, they were guided by focussed interview schedules. The people interviewed were:

Chief officers responsible for community service at a policy level.
Senior managers responsible for the day to day management of community service.
Community Service staff of all levels, i.e. probation officers, community service officers and sessional supervisors.
Offenders undertaking community service. A large sample was interviewed at the start of their community service order, with as many as possible also being interviewed at the end of their order.
Agency and Group Supervisors responsible for the projects chosen for detailed study.

Informal discussions also took place with all of the above groups, plus beneficiaries wherever this was possible.

Repertory Grids:

Two standard grids were devised for use within interviews. One was used with staff to elicit their views about a range of possible work projects on community service, and one for offenders working on community service. This latter grid was designed to elicit some of their views and understandings about themselves, and in particular to assess any change which might have occurred over the period of their order.

Questionnaires:

Two detailed questionnaires were devised, both for use with community service staff. The first was designed to establish the amount of time spent on a range of tasks within community service, and was used in the assessment of cost of community service. The second was a Likert scale, designed to obtain views about CS schemes, and give us some measure of job satisfaction.

Records Analysis:

A comprehensive analysis of the records of approximately 100 cases in each area was undertaken. Detailed data were extracted about all aspects of the cases:

- basic details about the order and sentence, the offences for which it was made, other sentences at the same time, comments of the sentencer, and any social inquiry report prepared.
- detailed information about the offender subject to the order, his/her race, gender, accommodation and employment histories.
- detailed information about the offender's progress through the order, his/her initial allocation to work, attendance, type of work undertaken, etc.
- information abut each individual breach and reconviction.
- information about completion of the order, nature of termination, time to complete, etc.

Research in practice

As with any large, complex research project, there were numerous unforseen issues which arose during the course of the research project: some large, some small; some unique to this project, some which highlight broader research issues. Whilst some of the practical problems experienced were interesting, often informative, and occasionally humorous, I feel that those problems which relate to the operationalisation of concepts within the research highlight more critical features for evaluation generally.

Social construction of key operational definitions

Creating operational definitions of key concepts is a critical aspect of any research project. In this research it proved to be no easy matter, with our initial definitions needing to be revised in the light of practical experience on the ground. Whilst this did create some problems for the research and the collection of data, the exercise of clarifying and refining the operational definitions helped us to develop our conceptual framework for understanding community service.

a) *'Community service scheme'*

When thinking about the unit of analysis for this research we initially planned to look at probation areas. We knew from previous experience however that one probation area can contain within it several different bases from which community service is operated. Sometimes all of these bases work in exactly the same way, but more often they work differently. Our notion of a 'Community Service Scheme' was one which incorporated some idea of common practice within it. In the end we decided that the one feature which could encapsulate this idea was the management unit of community service in an area: we decided that our definition of a scheme should be determined by the geographical area covered by an SPO or community service manager. This could be one small part of a county, the whole of a county, or something in between. In effect the areas where research was undertaken covered the full range of possibilities:

Scheme A: One scheme covered the whole of a probation area but operated from three different locations within it: a Senior Probation Officer was responsible for the day to day management of CS for the whole of the county, being based in the largest CS centre and travelling to the other two as necessary. The senior had a team of three probation officers, each of whom was responsible for one of the locations.

Scheme B: This scheme covered one division of a probation area, with one main administrative centre but several reporting sites within the division. A community service manager was responsible for the whole of the division, having a team of four community service officers, each of whom was responsible for a small geographical section of the division.

Scheme C: One large city was covered by this scheme, which was managed by a senior probation officer with three probation officers working from the same base.

Scheme D: One division of a large metropolitan city was covered by this scheme. It was managed by one full time and one part time senior probation officer, with three probation officers, all working from the same city centre office.

Scheme E: This was the 'scheme' which was hardest to define. Day-to-day responsibility for the management of community service lay with the field team seniors, with one probation officer in each team directly running community service either full time or part time. Co-ordination of community service within the county was the functional responsibility of one senior probation officer who met with probation officers running CS and their field seniors on a regular basis. There were too many teams within the county to be covered by the research, and we decided to include 3 teams which were felt to be representative of the range of teams in the area. We never really decided whether to define our coverage here as 3 separate schemes or part of a large scheme!

b) *'Community service project'*

When beginning this research, we thought we knew what a 'project' was in relation to community service - it identified one particular task or job which would be undertaken by a group of community service workers. It would be the work unit to which offenders were allocated to work. In practice we discovered wide variation on the ground. Some schemes did indeed allocate workers in this way, but many had other ways. One scheme allocated workers to a work day, with the details of exactly which group, supervisor and job being decided when they reported for work on that day. Another scheme allocated workers to a type of task, for instance gardening, but again the supervisor and specific job would be decided on reporting. Yet another scheme allocated workers to a supervisor, with the specific details of the task changing. There was also evidence that some schemes used a variety of methods within it.

This created particular difficulties for the quantitative analysis of case records, especially with deciding whether a worker had changed project or not.   In some it was very clear that their work allocation had changed in some way, but in others it was unclear from the record whether they were still reporting to the same 'project' but the specific task of that project had changed.   In the end we had to go with the local scheme's definition of a 'project' and try to identify within that scheme whether the work allocation had changed.   This was made easier by employing a research assistant in each area who came to understand the workings of that area and thus more readily identify some change.

c) *'Failure to attend' (fta)*

To an outsider it would seem to be very clear what constitutes a failure to attend for work: it occurs when someone has been told they should turn up for work and has failed to do so.   In these very clear circumstances there was no problem of definition.   However, problems arose for two reasons: the first was when the circumstances were not so clear, and the second was that recording practice varied considerably between schemes.   The problem was made more difficult by the introduction of national standards for community service early in our research, which required that all failures to attend must be designated as 'acceptable' or 'unacceptable'.

The example of a worker giving notice of a holiday and being given permission to take it provides useful illustration.   In one of the schemes the holiday date would be recorded as a failure to attend with an acceptable reason: in another area it would be recorded with 'Excused' by the date, whilst in yet another that date would not be recorded at all as there was no expectation that the worker would be reporting.   Sometimes failures to attend were retrospectively recorded as 'Excused' rather than as acceptable failures to attend.   One area was particularly keen on punctuality, and had a rule that if a worker reported late they would be sent home and this would be recorded as a failure to attend; however, it would only count as half a failure for the purposes of deciding whether to initiate breach proceedings!

Another practice complication was what happened when breach proceedings had been initiated.   In one scheme the practice was that the regular allocation of work was still open to the offender and thus was recorded as such and a failure to attend occurred if the worker awaiting a breach hearing did not turn up.   In another scheme there was no expectation that the worker would turn up for work, and thus this was not recorded as a failure; if the worker did decide to work this was allowed and was recorded as an attendance.   The former scheme inevitably had higher rates of FTA because of its recording practice.

Follow up action for failure to attend was very difficult to ascertain from many records. Frequently the action would be to wait for the next appointment and seek an explanation then if the worker turned up. If he or she did not then a visit or a letter would follow, but this would then become the follow up action for both of the failures.

In view of these tremendous difficulties in practice we decided the data collected from this exercise was not comparable between schemes and thus was of little practical value despite the considerable investment of time and effort in its collection.

d) 'Cost of community service'

A significant element of the research was an assessment of the costs of community service (see Knapp et al., 1990 for a detailed description). To undertake this aspect a detailed breakdown of the spending on community service for the schemes covered by the research was required from each area. A form was devised showing the areas of spending for which information was required. Anticipating that the sophistication of financial systems would vary considerably between areas we had kept the list simple and outlined a number of items for which exact figures for the previous financial year were required.

On receipt of this request by the areas we discovered that things were far more complicated than anticipated. The net result of these complications were that (a) some items of cost were excluded completely because of the difficulties of ensuring comparability, eg the costs of buildings; (b) estimates had to be made in relation to some elements of expenditure, and (c) the categories within which we originally planned to collect information had to be collapsed further to ensure consistency across areas. This resulted in a final categorisation of Staff, Travel & Vehicles, Property & Office, and Equipment & Offenders. Even then there were still differences between areas which had an impact on comparability of costs and adjustments had to be made in the light of these. A few examples of the complications will illustrate.

(i) The costs of vehicles were particularly difficult to make comparable. Some areas hire their vans on a regular basis, some lease them, and others purchase them. Where vehicles are purchased there is a higher cost for the year of purchase but then allowance has to be made for depreciation of the vehicles over a number of years.

(ii) Some items of expenditure, e.g. sessional supervisors, could be easily identified within an area, but unfortunately could not be split down to subsections within an area.   This meant that where we required information from just a section of the area precise details were not available and estimates had to be made.   Where information was available this estimation was made on the proportion of the whole area's community service orders which were made in the parts being researched.

(iii) Some items of expenditure could not be identified specifically for community service in some areas. For instance stationery and furniture are often costed to one central budget from which an estimate had to be made for expenditure on community service.

(iv) Some areas had costs not applicable to other areas, eg one area used external solicitors to prosecute breaches rather than community service staff. This cost was therefore included as a staff cost for comparability.

Overall, the view of our consultant for this component of the research, Martin Knapp, was that the adjustments and calculations made were the best which would be done in the circumstances   The overwhelming majority of cost of community service came from staffing, which had least problems, and thus the cost adjustments in other areas which may create inconsistency would be marginal in their eventual impact on cost per order and their comparison.

e) 'Race'

We were concerned to address equal opportunity issues within the research design, and thus included a requirement to collect information about race and gender for each offender in the quantitative sample. Research purposes required that the assessment should be made by community service staff - it was their involvement with the offenders which was being assessed, and this would be based on their own judgement of the offender's race.   Rather naïvely, we were not prepared for the responses which came back from some of the schemes involved in response to our request for this information. At that time race and ethnic monitoring was not routinely undertaken by every probation service in a standard way and we required race to be categorised as Asian, Afro-Caribbean, or White. Research experience at that time (and still) shows that there are critical differences between the experiences of Black Asian and Black African/Caribbean offenders.
    Two probation services had an agreed local policy about the collection of race information from offenders, and because of this would not allow information to be collected in any other way, even as a one-off limited exercise.   The information they collected was self reported, and from one

area was on the basis of Black/White only. Both these areas, and one other which collected probation officer perception of race, had a system for obtaining this information at pre-sentence report stage for recording this data within their local information systems and required us to use this information. The other two areas were happy for community service staff to make the assessment on the researcher's basis.

In the light of these controversies we had to compromise on the data. The information which was eventually collected was not strictly speaking comparable across the areas. All the data were condensed to Black/White even if provided in more detail, and the source of the information was mixed: some came from the offender, some from the probation officer who prepared the pre-sentence report, and some from the community service staff.

Deconstructing accepted constructs

a) *'Successfully completed order'*

Strictly speaking a successfully completed order is one where the offender works off the full number of hours ordered by the court. However, this definition covers a wide range of circumstances. At one end of the spectrum is the 'ideal' where the community service worker starts the order promptly, attends as requested, is never absent, never questioned about performance, and quickly completes the hours ordered. At the opposite end is the 'just made it' community service order, where the offender has difficulty in completing the hours ordered. Frequently failing to attend this offender will often provide medical certificates to cover absences; there may have been one or even two breaches proved in court and the order allowed to continue. The offender eventually completes the required hours after the court has been requested to allow the order to extend beyond the normal 12 month time limit. This type of offender frequently knows how to play the community service 'game', keeping just within allowable boundaries but creating much hassle and extra work for community service supervisors and staff in the process.

Another scenario is one were the offender has been working well on community service and learning from the experience, but before the order is completed is sentenced to custody for an offence committed before being given community service. Strictly speaking this is an unsuccessful order because it would be revoked for reconviction, but in many ways it was very successful.

In our analysis of the data we decided against devising a classification of successes, but instead opted to describe the nature of successes in some detail.

b) *Group projects and individual placements*

Literature about community service frequently discusses the nature of the work which is undertaken by the offenders in terms of two main types of tasks: group and individual. These two categories have a string of associations attached to them:

Group:	*Individual:*
Industrialised	Community based
Uncaring	Caring
Physically demanding	Mentally/socially demanding
No beneficiary contact	Beneficiary contact
Disciplined	Relaxed
Menial	Worthwhile
Probation supervisor	Agency supervisor

Common understandings viewed the two types of work as distinct dichotomous categories - one or the other. When exploring these concepts on the ground, we discovered that they were in no way so clear cut. We discovered projects where offenders worked together in groups in the community undertaking 'caring' work with substantial beneficiary contact, for example lunch clubs, gardening projects and wheelchair shopping. We also found examples of individual agency placements where the offender was undertaking menial tasks and had no contact at all with beneficiaries.

We thus felt that group v individual was a false dichotomy and the concepts of 'group project' and 'individual placement' had no validity. We instead focused on describing the range of situations which we experienced in practice.

Messages for evaluating effectiveness

So, what were the results of the research? Did we evaluate success and identify criteria linked to it? Well, yes and no. In 1986 I devised an exercise for a workshop about community service at the ACOP Conference. It used a range of hypothetical figures for four fictional community service schemes, the aim being to show that judgements about 'good' schemes depended on the criteria being used by the judge as to which characteristics were most important. Among the group of participants, mainly chief and assistant chief probation officers, there was disagreement as to which was the 'best' scheme using the information available. At the end of this research we have ended up in much the same position. We can produce a similar table (see Hine and Thomas, 1996), but this time with real figures and real probation areas rather than hypothetical. The position we are in however, is the same as that of the participants of the workshop. What we have from this research, additional to the figures in the table, is the qualitative work which enabled researchers to gain a different perspective on effectiveness. We could thus say something about the way in which beneficiary agencies perceived their local schemes and offenders for instance. The research did more to clarify understandings of the complexities and competing perspectives of community service than in identifying criteria linked to success.

> ... if one wishes to evaluate ... community service and the rest - it does little good to do so on a single plane and in relation to a single value. Instead one must think of it as a complex institution and evaluate it accordingly, recognising the range of its penal and social functions and the nature of its social support. (Garland, 1990, p.290)

Social research does not take place in a vacuum - it occurs within a complex social and political context. The complexity described by Garland was well known to the researchers, and the challenge was how to produce a research design which was sensitive to internal probation service issues, and yet at the same time encompassed perspectives of these other stakeholders.

At the time of designing the research project we did not consciously follow a particular research model - something which in theory (though probably not in practice) is contrary to accepted academic wisdom.

The project is clearly Administrative Criminology in Hudson's terms (1993). It was 'applied research aimed primarily at assisting criminal justice and penal system professionals in policy development and decision making' (p.5), and its funding did 'arise from practice and policy concerns rather than the concerns of scholarly curiosity or theoretical debate' (p.6), although some of the personal interests of the researchers may have been classified as scholarly curiosity. In describing studies in relation to race and criminal justice which fit under this banner, Hudson implies inadequacy of this approach because it has 'contributed little to racial justice or to criminological understanding' (p.12). This may be so in relation to race issues, but I do not believe it is a necessary corollary of administrative criminology per se. The administrative evaluation of many penal initiatives has highlighted the inadequacies of the theories and ideologies on which they are based.

Our project was heavily influenced by Smith and Cantley's model of pluralistic evaluation (1988), which is neatly described by Cheetham et al. (1992):

> Perhaps most importantly, traditional evaluation demands an assumption of consensus, or unity among all parties within an organisation. Agreed criteria of success can then be defined and the extent to which these are attained can be measured. Pluralistic evaluation acknowledges that consensus is absent, and rather than struggling to force the illusion on unwilling subjects brings centre stage the multiple, possibly conflicting criteria of success of different parties to the process. (p.33)

My previous experiences of evaluating effectiveness within the probation service and of undertaking the ACOP national survey made me very well aware of the need to consider 'effectiveness' from the perspective of the range of stakeholders and their different objectives for community service. I joined a team with similarly committed views within a Department where one of the drafters of pluralistic evaluation (Cantley) was then working. It is perhaps therefore particularly surprising that we did not at the time consciously acknowledge the evaluative framework within which we were working, which did:

> ...identify the major constituent groups to the policy initiative and, throughout the research, compare them with each other, both in the ideological perspectives that they hold and their operational strategies. (Smith and Cantley, p.124)

The more recent writing of Pawson and Tilley (1994) describes a evaluation model called 'scientific realism'. The fundamental premise of this paper is that it is not enough to find out whether a project is effective or not. To be useful and have results which are valuable outside of the specific project the evaluation should be able to say something about *why* the project was or was not effective. This requires the researcher to specify the mechanisms through which it is anticipated the project will produce its effect and to build the means of assessing these into the research design. It 'starts with a *theory* of what makes programmes work and a *theory* of the circumstances in which such ideas are likely to be efficacious' (p.292 - emphasis in original).

Some elements of this were undertaken in the planning stages of our research when we drew complex diagrams including all the factors which we thought might have an effect on outcome and the relationships between these, and maybe with hindsight more of this thinking could have been built into the research design. For instance, proponents of the 'disciplined' approach to community service say that an immediate and authoritative response to early failures to attend will lead to more successful completions of orders. We found that the general attendance rate was marginally better in such areas, but that they processed more breaches. In terms of overall successful completions there was little difference, but the revocations were for failure to attend for community service rather than for reconviction. Our qualitative work suggests that there was a cost to this, both in financial terms (average of £1319 to process a breach across the areas), and in social terms for staff who had to handle the dilemmas raised by having to take breach action against offenders who may have contravened their order in letter but not necessarily in spirit (for instance a female offender who was breached for non-attendance because she was ill following an abortion and had not wanted to go to her doctor for a medical certificate).

All of the models of evaluation identified above acknowledge the complexity of the task of evaluative social research, particularly in the interpretation of results and their meaning for practice. Having undertaken this project I can only agree that the evaluation of effectiveness is no easy matter, even when just one criterion for effectiveness could be used. When evaluating an area of work such as community service where so many definitions of 'success' exist because of its wide range of stakeholders with differing criteria, and where so may factors can influence each 'success', a pluralist realist approach to the task provides hope of throwing real illumination on the topic.

The complexities of evaluation of work by probation officers with offenders has long been recognised, for instance Folkard (1981) in considering the evaluation of the IMPACT experiments said:

> ...evaluation may be more complex in probation than in other forms of social work, since probation officers are social workers as well as officers of the court, and evaluation of their work requires consideration of criteria related to social and criminal justice. ... long term objectives in penology are problematic, in that there is disagreement about what they should be, doubts about whether they can be achieved, and great difficulties of evaluation. (p.101)

Times have changed and, as quoted from David Faulkner (1989), probation officers should no longer be considered social workers, however the competing objectives of social and criminal justice still exist. Current trends in evaluation with its limited focus on reconviction as a measure of effectiveness are troubling many researchers. For instance, Raynor (1996) expresses his concern and suggests:

> ... research on effectiveness should be understood and undertaken not simply as a technical aid to efficient services, but as an active contribution to the improvement and reform of criminal justice. (p.191).

The impetus for reconviction evaluation comes not just from governmental funding of research which fits this description, but also from managers and practitioners within the probation service fighting to (a) work efficiently within increasingly reduced resources and rising workloads, and (b) to demonstrate that the intervention of the probation service in the lives of offenders does indeed achieve some useful purpose. Currently the reduction of re-offending is the prime definition of effectiveness. Those of us undertaking this sort of evaluation should strive to ensure that other outcome measures and some assessment of process are included in our research design to check that the pursuit of criminal justice objectives does not compromise social justice.

References

Adair, H., Harman, J. and Hine, J. (1987), *Community Service in the 80's: report of the ACOP National Community Service Survey*, ACOP, Wakefield.

Association of Chief Officers of Probation (1983), *Community Service Practice Guide*, ACOP, Wakefield.

Cheetham, J., Fuller, R., McIvor, G. and Petch, A. (1992*)*, *Evaluating Social Work Effectiveness*, Open University Press. Buckingham.

Faulkner, D.E.R. (1989), 'Future of the Probation Service: A View from the Government', *Justice of the Peace*, 23 September 1989, *Vol 153*, 606-607.

Folkard, S. (1991), 'Second Thoughts on IMPACT' in E.M.Goldberg and N. Connelly (eds.), *Evaluative Research in Social Care*, Heinemann, London.

Garland, David (1990*)*, *Punishment and Modern Society: A Study in Social Theory*, Oxford University Press, Oxford.

Hine, J. and Thomas, N. (1996), 'Evaluating work with Offenders: Community Service Orders',. in G. McIvor (ed.), *Working with Offenders*, Jessica Kingsley Publishers, London.

Home Office (1970), *Non-custodial and Semi-custodial Penalties.* (Report of the Advisory Council on the Penal System - Chair Baroness Wootton), HMSO, London.

Home Office (1988), *Punishment, Custody and the Community*, Cm424. Home Office, London.

Home Office (1989), *National Standards for Community Service Orders.* HOC18/89, Home Office, London.

Hudson, B. (1993), 'Racism and Criminology, Concepts and Controversies'. in D. Cook, and H. Hudson, (eds.), *Racism & Criminology*, Sage, London.

Knapp, M., Thomas, N. and Hine, J. (1990), 'The Economics of Community Service Orders: *A Study of Costs in Five English Areas'. Discussion Paper 697/92.* Personal Social Services Research Unit, University of Kent at Canterbury.

McIvor, G. (1992), *Sentenced to Serve: the operation and impact of community service by offenders*, Avebury, Aldershot.

Pawson, R. and Tilley, N. (1994), 'What Works in Evaluation Research?' *British Journal of Criminology, 34*, No 3, Summer 1994, 291-306.

Pease, Ken & McWilliams, William (1980),. *Community Service by Order*, Scottish Academic Press, Edinburgh.

Pease, K. (1983), 'Penal Innovations' in J. Lishman, (ed.), *Social Work with Adult Offenders: Research Highlights 5*, Aberdeen People's Press, Aberdeen.

Raynor, P. (1996), 'Effectiveness Now: A Personal and Selective Overview' in G. McIvor (ed.), *Working with Offenders: Research Highlights in Social Work 26*, Jessica Kingsley Publishers, London.

Rutherford, A. (1993), *Twenty Years of Community Service*, Paper to conference of same name 11.11.93, ACOP.

Smith, D. (1996),. 'Social Work and Penal Policy' in G. McIvor (ed.), *Working with Offenders: Research Highlights in Social Work 26*, Jessica Kingsley Publishers, London.

Smith, G. and Cantley, C. (1984),. 'Pluralistic Evaluation' in J. Lishman (ed.), *Evaluation: Research Highlights in Social Work 8*, Jessica Kingsley Publishers, London.

Thomas, N., Hine, J. and Nugent M. (1990*)*, *Study of Community Service Orders: Summary Report*, Department of Social Policy & Social Work, University of Birmingham.

West, J. (1976), 'Community Service Orders' in J.F.S. King (ed.), *Control Without Custody*, University of Cambridge, Cambridge.

Wright, M (1984), *In the Interests of the Community: A Review of the Literature on Community Service Orders*, University of Birmingham, Birmingham.

Young, W. (1979), *Community Service Orders: The Development and Use of a New Penal Measure*, Heineman, London.

ACKNOWLEDGEMENTS

I am grateful to Neil Thomas for his help in developing some of the initial ideas for this paper, which is based on my experience of undertaking the National Study of Community Service Orders with Neil Thomas and Mike Nugent at the University of Birmingham between 1988 and 1990. The report of the research was published by the Department of Social Policy & Social Work, University of Birmingham (Thomas et al., 1990).

8 Evaluating intensive probation: the American experience

Todd R. Clear

Los Angeles County (California) Chief Probation Officer, Barry Nidorf, upon considering the high rates of revocations in his Intensive Supervision Project (ISP), explained the findings in this way:

> As I begin to look at the effectiveness of my ISP program, I question whether recidivism rates--the number of offenders who return to crime--are really an appropriate measure... If community safety is the primary goal, then perhaps an arrest and revocation should be seen as an arrest and not a failure. (Nidorf, in Petersilia and Turner, 1991)

Herein lies a dilemma: Mr. Nidorf is almost certainly correct in that revocations are credible responses to violations of court orders. And yet, his point leads to an equally certain illogic. If revocations indicate effective probation, would a project in which the revocation rate is 100 per cent be regarded as 100 per cent effective?

The idea that revocation is a good thing, taken to its logical extreme, is absurd. Any ISP that revokes 100 per cent of its clients cannot, by any measure, be considered a success. So touting the high rate of revocations as an advertisement for a program's value seems almost obviously irrational.

Does this mean that a prerequisite to success is a low rate of revocation? Possibly, but a low revocation rate may not necessarily signify a successful ISP, either. Most observers would agree that intensive supervision programs are meant for high-risk offenders - why else would close monitoring make sense? Some have speculated that intensive programs with low revocation rates achieve them by admitting low-risk clients who are not appropriate for intensive supervision. (Clear and Hardyman, 1990).

The 'goals' problem

It seems a simple enough problem. To know how well a program works, the logical idea is to observe how well offenders perform within those programs. In good programs, offenders will do well; in bad ones, they will fail. How can it be that high rates of program failure lead to claims of success, while low failure rates provoke skepticism?

The answer has to do with the complex array of goals that ISPs are expected to achieve. In most programs in the United States, intensive supervision is not merely a way to deal with certain offenders more fittingly; ISP is also supposed to solve certain chronic and systemic problems within the prison and probation systems. It is also expected to advance manifest professional and organizational goals. Normally, ISP goals with regard to prison and probation effectiveness are stated openly; the internal goals related to the profession are less public.

In the USA, the manifest goals for intensive supervision programs are:

* Increase public safety
* Ensure adequate punishment
* Reduce prison crowding
* Save tax dollars

This is a complex array of goals going well beyond a simple expectation of low recidivism rates. The complexity of the goals of ISP has its origins in the circumstances under which these programs were developed. Two dominant forces shaped the development of intensive probation in the USA: extensive prison crowding and disrespect for the credibility of probation as a response to offending. The design of ISP was an intentional way to respond to these two forces.

Prison overcrowding was clearly a fiscal issue, but it also raised serious correctional program concerns. As the United States began to more than quadruple its prison capacity from 1971 to 1993, the cost of new prison construction began to alarm government fiscal planners. Moreover, local jails, even brand new jails just opened, were strangled with overcrowding, and resulting court ordered limits on jail populations forced release of some types of inmates who ordinarily would have been incarcerated awaiting trial. Over-crowding was regarded as a crisis that constrained choices in the use of tax revenues and detracted from overall correctional effectiveness.

Probation's lack of credibility also had both programmatic and fiscal implications. In programmatic terms, probation had lost its philosophical anchor. Doubts about the effectiveness of probation rehabilitation programs had seeped into the daily work attitudes of probation officers themselves (Harris and Clear,

1989), but other ways to confront offenders seemed elusive. Fiscally, years of level or reduced funding coupled with rampant growth in clients meant that caseloads nearly doubled in a scant ten years. (Austin and Killman, 1990) One expert referred to probation as 'a kind of standing joke.' (Martinson, 1976)

Into this breach strode probation administrators, with a promise that both problems could be solved with a new, tough version of probation: ISP. The ISP solution seemed on its face promising for several reasons. First, it was axiomatic that probation of any sort was cheaper than prison of any sort. Thus, since an offender's punishment requires public resources, why not inexpensive probation rather than the comparatively prohibitive prison? Similarly, this new, tough version of probation would preempt the need for prison expansion, since offenders otherwise considered too risky could be managed under ISP in the community. This would save precious prison space for the truly dangerous offender, and it would once and for all demonstrate the credibility of community-based punishments, properly funded.

These aims have proven elusive. The most sophisticated evaluations of ISP have been conducted by a Rand researcher team, led by Joan Petersilia (Petersilia and Turner, 1990a) , but their results do not differ substantially from those of other, less methodologically rigorous evaluations (Clear and Braga, 1995; Tonry and Lynch, 1995). The normal bottom-line of these studies is not very promising: compared to control groups, ISP offenders do not have fewer arrests nor does their supervision cost less. In fact, Mr. Nidorf's defense above of his ISP program - one of the several evaluated by the Rand studies - was a response to the negative findings about the value of ISP in his agency.

The profession has found these results difficult to accept, because on the face of it, the ISP claims seem unassailable. Prison seems undeniably more expensive than close supervision in the community. Risk seems obviously lessened by tighter supervision and more effective surveillance. Probation officials find the ISP bottom line suspicious, and wonder how it can be true. Their doubts are supported by the fact that ISPs continue to proliferate in the face of the Rand studies and others like them.

The context for ISP failure

The reasons ISP evaluations turn up such unsupportive results lies in an understanding of the sociopolitical context of their program design and implementation, especially as they relate to prison populations and local politics. The unique character of US experience with ISP can be explained in terms of four dynamics: prison populations, local politics, program design and program implementation.

To fully understand the US experience, we must begin with a recognition that unlike European countries, crime control policy in the United States is the province of local governments. State legislatures write penal codes and run prison systems. Probation is often a county-level agency, administered by the courts. Arrests are primarily performed by municipal law enforcement agencies.

The fact that crime control is so localized means that there are really no national standards for ISP. In fact, each ISP program is its own story, and what may be true about one ISP is often untrue about another. The localized focus of penal policy has at least two other ramifications. First, those who would design an ISP have as their stakeholder audience persons with whom they have frequent contact. This makes it easy for seemingly tangential agendas to become attached to the design and implementation of ISPs. Second, the distribution of costs and benefits among local audiences is not always obvious. When counties run probation, the incentives for saving state prison costs are diluted at best.

With these observations in mind, let us discuss four aspects of the ISP implementation context in the USA.

Prison populations

The demography of the prison population is important for the simple reason that if the ISP is to save money, offenders who would ordinarily be in prison instead must be placed in the community. Obviously, ISP is not cheaper than regular probation. If offenders are not diverted from prison onto ISP, costs of the new ISP will represent budget increases.

Finding offenders in prison (or bound for prison) who are suitable for ISP is made difficult by the fact that rearrest risk and current crime seriousness are not highly correlated (Gottfredson and Gottfredson, 1986). So-called violent offenders often do very well in the community, and may have a rearrest probability that is quite low. But to design ISPs for offenders convicted of violent crimes is, as we shall see, a political impracticality.

Thus, within the prison population, there are three types of ISP-relevant offenders. There are those convicted of violent crimes who might do well in a non-secure environment. There are nonviolent offenders who have persisted in committing offenses, thus leading to a prison term. And there are drug offenders. Each of these groups presents problems for the ISP administrator who would target them for a program. Serious offenders are a political risk, while petty recidivists and drug offenders have high rates of noncompliance with the law, and therefore are management problems in a probation caseload. Neither of these problems is insurmountable, but they require a credible programmatic and professional basis on which public trust can be built. Because probation systems often lacked this credibility, the 'target group' problem posed serious dilemmas for probation administrators.

Local politics

In the USA, local politics are dominated by a clash between two themes: getting tough on crime and reducing the tax burden. Until recently, these were not conflicting ideals; the total proportion of the state budget devoted to corrections was often as low as 3-5 per cent. But after a twenty year period of prison expansion, correctional budgets have soared, and in some states promise to be 20 per cent of the budget or even more. Even a small percentage of state budgets can be devastating, since much of what a state spends in its overall budget is 'mandatory' costs that cannot be avoided, such as retirement benefits or welfare. All correctional costs must be taken from the 'discretionary' portion of the state budget, which also funds schools, roads, and so forth.

This leads to a natural desire to restrict the growth of the corrections budget in order to protect other funding priorities. When ISP promises to do so, it draws attention from local political leaders.

But local politics also places constraints upon correctional reform. The main constraint is the symbolic value of the prison sentence. When the community gets outraged about a particular type of conduct, making it susceptible to prison (or to *longer terms* in prison) symbolizes public rebuke.

If this is so, then political leaders cannot be blamed for thinking that to reduce susceptibility to prison is to invite public symbols of acceptance of the behaviour. For example, an entirely suitable type of offender for ISP might be someone who has been convicted of selling drugs. But in the 1980s environment of 'zero-tolerance' for drug use, releasing such offenders to ISP might be seen as equivocal about the symbolic response to such crimes.

Therefore, political interests severely restrict ISP populations in ways that mere programmatic concerns might not. Those convicted of violence are ineligible due to the seriousness of their crimes; drug offenders are excluded on similar criteria. Repeat offenders of less-serious crimes are eligible, but their lengthy records make them poor risks for ISP. And their (often) short sentences mean they do not result in much overall savings in bed space when sent to ISP instead of prison.

Program design.

After all this discussion, it may seem ironic that most ISPs in the USA are not designed to divert offenders from prison. Two sentencing realities make it possible for ISPs to avoid custody-bound offenders: sentencing disparity and the tradition of long sentences.

Disparity in sentencing means that some offenders who are sentenced to community penalties look very much like some offenders sentenced to prison (or jail). ISPs that profile these offenders (often low-level recidivists but also sometimes drug offenders) may be successful in getting these offenders sentenced to their programs, but they cannot be certain that the offenders would not have been on some other form of probation instead.

Long sentences also impede true diversion of cases from prison, for it seems a much more radical shift in practice to sentence a case to ISP when the prison sentence would have been, say, 15 years. The fact that only a fraction of that sentence would actually have been served - as little as 10 per cent in some places - is the irony. In the US, there is good evidence that the percentage of a judicial sentence that is actually served has been dropping for the last three decades, not because the time served is dropping (actual time served appears to be level or increasing) but because, the sentences imposed by judges have been inflating dramatically. Thus, at sentencing, judges are often faced with making a public choice between a community sentence and a term of a half-decade or longer in prison. All the system's actors know that the latter sentence is something of a mirage created for public consumption, but they are ironically impeded from conveying the relative harshness of the ISP alternative by the charade of the penal sentence - even though offenders know the truth and sometimes opt for prison instead of ISP, because the former is easier time and sometimes even *shorter* time (Petersilia and Turner, 1990b).

So ISP programs find it easier politically and practically to target probation cases instead of prison cases. This tendency in ISPs has led to the coining of an adjective to describe most ISP programs, by their design as 'probation enhancement ISPs.' The point is that they operate as an alternative to probation, not prison.

Program implementation

ISPs have been implemented as no-nonsense 'tough' correctional programs. Conditions of probation ordered by the judge are often both onerous and numerous, and they are stringently enforced. This provides the ISP program with good rhetoric for public consumption: 'In our ISP you are going to be subjected to tough standards of behaviour, and you are going to be watched closely to insure you are meeting those standards.' (This is precisely the conceptual language used to define 'boot camps,' as though ISPs are community-located boot camps.)

With virtually any offending population, a combination of tough program requirements and strict enforcement of those rules has a predictable result: clients are discovered to be in noncompliance. These clients then become 'program failures'; many are removed from the ISP program and placed in confinement.

The goals of ISP

The ISP context goes a long way toward explaining the main research findings about the success of these programs in meeting their goals.

Increase public safety

It is no doubt unrealistic to expect any correctional program to alter appreciably the level of public safety, but this must be especially true for ISPS. There are 35 million serious crimes a year in the United States; yet less than 4 million offenders are under correctional supervision in the community. Of these, the number under ISP at any given time is probably no more than 10,000. Even if these programs are stupendously effective at preventing crime among their clients, the aggregate impact on crime rates would be unnoticeable.

The evidence is pretty good that these programs are not stupendously successful at preventing crime. The Rand studies (Petersilia and Turner, 1990a, 1992) find no significant impact of ISP on rates of clients' arrest. This result is repeated in other studies carried out in Georgia (Erwin, 1984), Ohio (Latessa and Vito, 1988), Massachusetts (Byrne and Kelley, 1989) and New Jersey (Pearson, 1987). It seems unassailable that ISP, at least as has been practiced in the USA, holds little promise of reducing the rate of return to criminality among its clients.

Three caveats must be taken to this argument. First, while it seems clear that the *prevalence* of criminality is unaffected by ISP, some have speculated that the *incidence* of crime may be reduced. That is, the proportion who engage in crime may be the same, but their levels of engagement in crime and the duration of activity before they are intercepted may be smaller, due to ISPs greater level of surveillance (Petersilia and Turner, 1990a).

Second, the Rand studies have shown that ISP may increase rates of retention in drug treatment programs. It is known that the length of time in drug treatment is associated with successfully avoiding relapse into drug use, and that when relapse is avoided new criminality is avoided. (Ball, Shaffer and Nurco, 1983) This has led some to speculate that the long range agenda for ISP ought to be found in its ability to further rehabilitation goals. (Gendreau, Cullen and Bonta, 1994; Byrne and Kelly, 1989)

Third, a small but impressive set of studies suggest that good case management practices, especially with higher risk offenders, are associated with improved performance under supervision, including fewer arrests. (Markley and Eisenberg, 1987; Baird, Heinz and Bemus, 1979; Andrews and Bonta, 1993) There can be no question that, with reduced caseloads, ISP officers have an enhanced capacity for effective case management, should they choose to use their time this way.

Perhaps. But the USA's ISP programs have not, in the general case, been anxious to adopt intervention principles that seem to be associated with successful treatment outcomes or effective case management (see Andrews and Bonta, 1993). At least one study found that the ISP program's philosophy about service-delivery versus surveillance functions translated directly into staff behaviours with cases (Clear and Latessa, 1993). Most ISPs are unabashedly control-oriented in their language and policy.

Thus, the capacity for ISP to enhance public safety to any meaningful degree is thwarted by numbers alone. But even the small contribution that *could* be made by these programs is hampered by political contexts which seem to force an over-reliance on practices of surveillance and control, inability to target the truly high risk offender who is best situated to benefit from interventions, and the inadequate use of sound intervention principles in the supervision of offenders.

Ensure adequate punishments

ISPs are an undeniably more stringent form of correctional control than probation - they provide a type of supervision that is more intrusive, inconvenient and burdensome than regular probation. The studies that show some jailed inmates would rather finish their sentences in confinement than be released to ISP (Petersilia and Turner, 1990a) suggest also that ISP can be more onerous than confinement. For those whose punitive tastes run to the extravagant, this is seen as a promising finding. The invention of a community-based penalty that challenges the prison in unpleasantness is an accomplishment indeed.

At the more mundane level, it may be argued that ISP, because it occurs in the community, affords a type of accountability that cannot accompany the institutional sentence: community service, restitution, fines and child support. In these areas, ISP is potentially superior both to prison and to traditional probation.

However, what is required to make a punishment 'adequate' lies largely in the eye of the beholder. In the USA, extreme sentences are so routine that the punitive value of ISP is preempted by comparison to prison sentences, even when ISP is acknowledged to be 'tough.' To be blunt, how can any program in the community compare in the symbolics of punitiveness to the moment in court when the judge says, 'I sentence you to 10 years in the state prison.' No matter that the 10 years in all probability amounts to far less than that, in practice. Inflation in the symbols of penality has watered down the ISP alternative.

As a result, there are no studies which indicate that the advent of ISP in a jurisdiction has meant the public feels offenders are being more effectively punished. It is true that focus group research methods have shown that citizens, when informed about ISP, will see it as punitive, but that merely suggests a potential for ISP to deliver on the punitive agenda, not an actual accomplishment.

In virtually every jurisdiction in the United States, prisons are crowded well beyond capacity, and this is true whether or not the jurisdiction has an ISP. Since even the largest ISP programs have capacities that are a mere fraction of the overall prison population in the corresponding state, it is hard to see how an argument can be framed that this goal has been achieved. No program has claimed to erase substantially the problem of crowding in its state's or county's institutions.

Nevertheless, several evaluation reports have made claims that ISPs have enabled jurisdictions to avoid some degree of new prison construction, notably in New Jersey (Pearson, 1987) and Georgia (Erwin, 1984). These claims are based upon assumptions, of course, and the primary assumption is this: a high percentage of program entrants would have gone to prison had the program not existed.

Any claim to certainty that a person who is on ISP would have otherwise been in prison can only be based upon shaky evidence. Even 'back-end' programs, such as New Jersey's ISP, are subject to net-widening, as it was reported some judges sentenced offenders to prison in the belief they would be quickly released to ISP (Clear and Hardyman. 1988). Front-end programs are even more susceptible to this kind of problem. In Georgia, judges sign an affidavit saying they would have put the person in prison without ISP, but insiders accept that the veracity of the assertion is often questionable.

Most states require only that a person be convicted of a crime for which prison is an *eligible* sanction to enable the judge to select ISP. Other states are more stringent, for example in Florida, if a guideline calls for a short prison sentence, the judge may impose a community control alternative. But even this is not fail-safe: prior to the Florida ISP, in many cases for which a short prison term was the guideline sentence, judges had a history of departing from the guideline and imposing probation anyway. Studies indicate that a portion of Florida's program entrants are true diversions from jail or prison, but the size of that portion is unclear (Baird, 1989).

The toughness of the ISP surveillance also seems to mitigate against the prison crowding agenda. Studies show that ISPs have high in-program failure rates. Many of these failures eventually wind up in prison, anyway, thus wiping out any savings in cell space. If the problem of net-widening is added into this formula, it means that perhaps some of these eventual prison entrants would have been on regular probation (with fewer conditions and less surveillance) instead of ISP. Rand's estimates (Petersilia and Turner, 1990a) are that ISP cases may actually end up spending *more* time in secure custody than the comparison group.

In order to save tax dollars, less money must be spent on punishing offenders. Nowhere in the United States are corrections budgets decreasing; indeed, everywhere these government budget items are escalating faster than just about any other line item, often including health care. This is true regardless of the size or scope of the ISP or related program in that jurisdiction. The advent of the ISP has not saved corrections from growing in cost.

It is hypothetically true that the ISPs could have reduced *potenti*al costs - and this is what is usually meant by the aim of saving tax dollars. Community penalties are cheaper to implement than institutional penalties, and so if they serve as an alternative, certain costs might be avoided.

The claim of tax savings is undercut by the fact that so many ISP clients are not being diverted from prison. ISP is up to ten times *more* expensive than regular probation. When it replaces regular probation, it is nearly impossible to save expenses.

The claim of saving tax dollars is made even more improbable by the tough enforcement policies incorporated into the programs. Rand's analysis of ISP shows that these costs can be considerable. Every case that 'fails' and goes to prison for the original sentence not only obliterates any potential savings, but also adds the costs of the ISP option that failed.

Even if all cases in an ISP are diversions, the programmatic toughness can eradicate the potential for savings. Let us say that an ISP 'costs' $5,000 per year, while prison 'costs' $20,000. A hundred cases getting two years on ISP then will cost one million dollars; these same cases getting a year in prison will cost $2 million. But if the ISP has a 50 per cent failure rate, and failures average 6 months on ISP and then serve their year in prison, then the ISP under these terms costs a total of $1.65 million. If only 80 per cent of the ISP cases are diverted from prison, the program costs of prison and ISP are essentially equal.

Some ISPs enforce their conditions by threatening a tariff for failures: the original sentence will be augmented by a penalty for the affront of having violated the 'last chance' option of ISP. People who argue for this policy do so in the hopes it will increase the credibility of the ISP program. If so, there is a price tag on that credibility. In the facts outlined above, a 33 per cent tariff for the program failures means that program costs approach equality even when all ISP program entrants are true diversions.

This example is farfetched in several regards. ISP cases seldom are in that status for two full years before they are declared 'successful.' On the other hand, no ISP program achieves anything close to a 100 per cent diversion rate (a 50 per cent diversion rate is often the most that a program will even claim). Moreover, the average prison sentence being avoided is often much less than a year more like six months. But even these changes are not helpful to the argument. A 6-month ISP program that costs $2,500 per offender and has a 50 per cent true diversion rate from prison sentences that would have averaged 6-months and cost $10, 000 per offender actually costs more total tax dollars as the failure rate begins to exceed 25 per cent, even without a failure tariff. Almost every ISP has a failure rate in excess of 25 per cent.

Discussion

A simple contextual evaluation of ISP programs and program assumptions might have indicated the improbability that ISP would be able to achieve its goals. The slippery slope of political necessity and practical reality militate against successful ISPs, at least if one is to take their manifest goals as criteria for success. The fact that evaluations confirm this sorry picture should not surprise us.

Why, then, have ISPs proliferated so widely?

One answer is that the stated goals of ISP are not necessarily the main criteria on which the ISP movement should be judged. This paper began by asserting the twin demons of penal administration in the USA: institutional overcrowding and lack of respect for community penalties. The stated goals of ISP relate almost exclusively to the former problem. If one takes the problem of demonstrating a feasible, effective community-based penalty as the basis for evaluating ISP, there are indications it has succeeded.

These indications do not lie in the public's eye, necessarily, but in the eyes of the system's insiders and funders. The very fact that ISPs proliferate is the evidence of their success.

This is far from tautological, though it may seem that way at first glance. ISPs are presented as an innovation dedicated to have impact on the external environment of the community corrections system: prison crowding, crime, and taxes. But what if the ISP story is recast to make it an innovation designed to alter the internal landscape of the corrections system, with regard to the strength and capacity of the community penalties themselves? Cohen (1985) has argued a similar theme: the purpose of the system's innovations are internally motivated, to grow stronger, deeper and more complex.

Faced with an endemic problem of low credibility in the USA, probation administrators found themselves increasingly irrelevant to the conversation about crime. Budgets were stagnant or even decreasing. Certainly, probation was not often asked to sit at the penal policy table. The penal conversation was about prisons.

By developing a new generation of 'tough' ISPs, probation administrators changed the conversation about their agencies, presented their function in a new light, and made for themselves a place at the policy table. A function that had been seen as outmoded came to be reconceptualized. No longer a puny version of pro-offender social work, probation, in its ISP rebirth, was now a crime-related, no-nonsense, pro-system agency. It embraced major goals of its sister law enforcement agencies - crime and even cost control-and it absorbed the dominant paradigm that crime is 'fought' and 'confronted.'

In this regard, accomplishment of the main goals is an added benefit. When agency directors were able to reincarnate their credibility with the system as indicated by growing budgets and growing demands for performance, the most important goals were actually accomplished.

When Barry Nidorf said that the 'probation failures' were more appropriately seen as program successes, he was really commenting on what the program was all about. Probation administrators wanted to be seen as unafraid of being stern with offenders, as not so much concerned with keeping offenders on the streets as with making then behave in certain ways while they were there. The evaluation results, and the reactions these results spawned, confirm the degree to which the field, in need of a new place in the scheme of corrections, helped to achieve it through ISP.

References

Andrews, D. and Bonta, J.B. (1993), *The Psychology of Criminal Conduct*, Anderson, Cincinnati.

Austin, J. and Killman, D. (1990), *NCCD Focus: America's Growing Correctional Industrial Complex*, National Council on Crime and Delinquency, San Francisco.

Baird, C.S. (1989), *Analysis of the Diversionary Impact of the Florida Community Control Program*, National Council on Crime and Delinquency, Madison.

Baird, C. S., Heinz, R. and Bemus, B.J. (1979), *The Wisconsin Staff Deployment/Case Classification Project: Two Year Follow-Up*, Wisconsin Department of Health and Human Services, Madison.

Ball, J. C., Shaffer, J. and Nurco, D. (1983), 'The Day-to-Day Criminality of Heroin Addicts in Baltimore: a Study in the Continuity of Offense Rates,' *Drug and Alcohol Dependence, 12*, 119-142.

Byrne, J. and Kelly, L. (1989), *Restructuring Probation as an Intermediate Sanction: An Evaluation of the Massachusetts Intensive Probation Supervision Program*. Final Report to the National Institute of Justice, MA: Univ. of Lowell, Lowell.

Clear, T.R. and Braga, A. (1995), 'Community Corrections', in J. Q. Wilson and J. Petersilia (eds.), *Crime*, Institute for Contemporary Studies, San Francisco.

Clear, T. R. and Hardyman, P. (1990), 'The New Intensive Supervision Movement', *Crime and Delinquency, 36*, 42-60.

Clear, T. R.. and Latessa, E (1993), 'Probation officers' Roles in Intensive Supervision: Surveillance vs. Treatment,' *Justice Quarterly, 10*, 441-462.

Cohen, S. (1985), *Visions of Social Control*. Cambridge: Polity.

Erwin, B. S., (1984*), Evaluation of Intensive Supervision in Georgia*, Department of Corrections, Atlanta, Georgia.

Gendreau, P., Cullen, J and Bonta, J. (1994), 'Intensive Rehabilitation Probation: The Next Generation in Community Corrections?', *Federal Probation, 58*, 72-78.

Gottfredson, D. and Gottfredson, D.M. (1986), 'Accuracy of Prediction Models', in A. Blumstein, J. Cohen, J. A. Roth, and C. Visher (eds.), *Criminal Careers and 'Career Criminals'*, National Academy Press, Washington, D.C.

Harris, P. M. and Clear, T. R. (1989), 'Have Probation and Parole Officers Changed Their Attitudes Toward Their Work?', *Justice Quarterly, 6*, 233-246.

Latessa, E.J. and Vito, G. Jr. (1988), 'The Effects of Intensive Supervision on Shock Probationers', *Journal of Criminal Justice, 16*, 319-330.

Markley, G. and Eisenberg, M. (1987), *Evaluation of Texas Parole Classification and Case Management system*, Texas Board of Pardons and Paroles, Austin.

Martinson, R. (1979), 'California Research at the Crossroads', *Crime and Delinquency 22*, 178-191.

Pearson, F. (1987), *Final Research on New Jersey's Intensive Supervision Program*, University Institute for Criminological Research, Rutgers, New Brunswick, NJ.

Petersilia, J. and Turner, S. (1990a), *Intensive Supervision for High-Risk Probationers: Results of Three California Experiments, Rand*, Santa Monica.

Petersilia, J. and Turner, S. (1990b), *Diverting Prisoners to Intensive Probation: Results of an Experiment in Oregon*, Rand, Santa Monica.

Petersilia, J. and Turner, S. (1991) 'An Evaluation of Intensive Probation in California', *The Journal of Criminal Law and Criminology, 82*, 610-658.

Tonry, M. and Lynch, M (1995), 'Intermediate Sanctions,' in N. Morris and M. Tonry (eds.), *Crime and Justice: An Annual Review*, University of Chicago, Chicago.

Turner, S. and J. Petersilia, J. (1992), 'Focusing on High-Risk Parolees: An Experiment to Reduce Commitments to the Texas Department of Corrections', *Journal of Research on Crime and Delinquency, 29*, 34-61.

9 The cost and cost effectiveness of community penalties: principles, tools and examples

Martin Knapp and Ann Netten

A price cannot be put on justice, but it is not without its costs

(Cm 965, 1990, para 9.1)

Introduction: demands and needs

Every public policy and every local decision in the criminal justice system and associated areas has an economic dimension. This has always been so, even if it has rarely been recognised. Costing policies and actions is just one facet of the economic dimension, for economics is a discipline which concerns itself, firstly and broadly, with *scarcity*, particularly its prevalence, sources and consequences, and secondly with the criteria for allocating scarce goods, services and resources. Thus economists are interested in the motivations and behaviours of individuals and groups, the structure and objectives of organisations, the implications of different resource allocations for the economic and general well-being of citizens, and ways to improve those allocations.

This chapter necessarily has a narrower focus than the broad economics of criminal justice issues: the focus is the evaluation of cost and cost-effectiveness of community penalties. We briefly examine the need for economic evaluations and offer a simple framework on which to build evaluations. Four basic evaluative principles are laid out, tools introduced, and their applications illustrated. Finally, we reflect briefly on the reasons for the marked shortage of economic evaluations of criminal justice services or policies.

The demand for cost and cost-effectiveness perspectives in the criminal justice area stems from needs which can be grouped under the headings of accountability, policy, practice and research. Accountability is probably the most familiar: costs, expenditure patterns, income streams, and service utilisation data are needed for the perennial performance reviews traditionally required for public probity. Today these are often built around value-for-money audits and efficiency scrutinies. As with the other demands described here, it needs careful combination of information from a variety of sources to provide the framework and evidence needed for accountability. There is also a need for a cost-effectiveness perspective at policy level, for example in planning criminal justice options, changes to sentencing guidelines or placement patterns, the creeping reliance on market forces in a variety of areas, and (semi-) privatisation of prison or escorting services. Central government and other decision makers must be aware of the resource effects of policy decisions. In some circumstances, these resource consequences may be the primary rationale for change, but even where they are not, it would be foolish to launch a new initiative or sanction a change of direction without awareness of the financial consequences.

At the practice level, many offenders receiving community penalties are supervised or supported by more than one agency. Community penalties sit in a complex inter-connected system of services and agencies. Coordination is especially important. There may yet be few moves towards devolved budgets or collaborative commissioning of the kind found in Britain's health and social care systems, but each practice decision - and this could include each sentencing decision by the courts - will have cost and cost-effectiveness consequences which agencies will want to identify.

Framework and principles

Ronald Reagan once offered a slightly unkind definition of an economist, even if it has a vein of accuracy: an economist sees something working in practice and then asks if it will work in theory. In fact, it is important to base any empirical evaluation, or any *reading* of an evaluation for the purposes of drawing out policy or practice implications, on a sound theoretical footing. This not only validates the evaluation but assists in the interpretation of findings. It also emphasises the complementarity of different research approaches - from criminology, economics, sociology, psychology or elsewhere.

In our own work we have often constructed practical evaluations around the *production of welfare framework*. The framework draws analogies between elements of mainstream economics - particularly cost and production relations - and the provision and impact of services (Knapp, 1984). It distinguishes between process or intermediate outputs, such as the numbers of people serving particular sentences or using a facility, and 'final outcomes', which are changes in the attributes and behaviour (including offending) of individual service users or the broader society. These outputs or outcomes are produced by combining resource inputs such as labour, capital and consumables, each with a price or cost. There are also 'non-resource inputs' which intervene between, and thus influence, the resources and outcomes. Examples would be the attitudes of

134

service users and the regime of a facility, demonstrating that non-resource inputs can be important determinants of the success or effectiveness of a service, sentence or facility, but that they do not have immediately identifiable prices or costs. The production of welfare framework is thus a helpful way to gather together (multi-disciplinary) arguments and evidence about the determinants of the effectiveness and cost of criminal justice activities or policies. It is a sound basis for building an economic evaluation.

The production of welfare framework is given a simplified representation in Figure 9.1. Hypothesised causal links, shown by arrows in the figure, require empirical investigation. Clearly, costs should not really be studied in isolation from other elements or dimensions. Indeed, this framework gives us some basic principles for cost or cost-effectiveness research:

- Costs should be comprehensively measured.

- The cost variations usually found between users, facilities, localities or sectors offer valuable information which should be explored and exploited.

- Variations encourage comparisons – this sentence type or group of offenders is more or less costly than that one - and these comparisons should be made on a like-with-like basis.

- Finally, cost information should be examined alongside information on outcomes.

These principles are easier to recite than to observe in practice, but they provide a useful framework for this chapter, and for marshalling and interpreting evidence. Our reason for describing them here is *not* to provide a step-by-step account of cost-effectiveness evaluation for the new researcher, or to convert everyone to economic terms and approaches, but to draw the attention of those people *using* cost information in their decision making to the need for *good quality* information which is appropriately employed. These four principles thus provide a benchmark for judging cost data and cost arguments.

Comprehensiveness

Principles

Many users of criminal justice services receive more than one service, probably from more than one agency. Someone on probation may also see a social worker, receive specialist support in relation to drug or alcohol misuse problems,

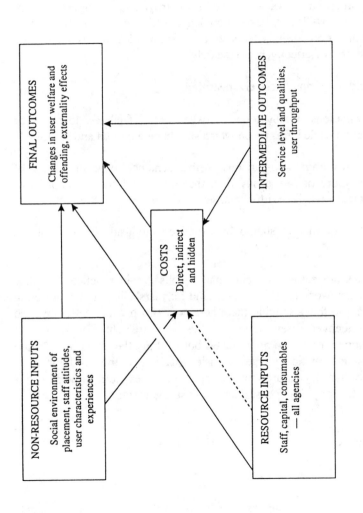

Figure 9.1: Production of welfare framework
Source: Based on Davies and Knapp (1981) and Knapp (1984)

and depend on financial assistance from social security payments. The greater and more diverse an individual's or family's needs, the broader the range of services utilised. An evaluation should aim to cost every one of these services. Even if the aim of an evaluation is simply to compare the costs of running, say, public and private prisons or large and small bail hostels, it would be dangerous to define costs narrowly to exclude services other than the prison or hostel, for there could be many implications for families, psychiatry, probation and after-sentence support, all of which could be affected by the way that prisons or hostels are run. A simple example is that a prison or hostel providing more services 'in-house' may appear more costly but will draw less on services such as probation.

Making sensible comparisons and ensuring that new service or sentencing developments are adequately funded are also compelling reasons for comprehensiveness. For example, innovative schemes such as reparation and mediation introduced by highly motivated individuals, often rely on time outside working hours or not included in line budgets. If the costs of such inputs are not included then comparing the costs and outcomes with mainstream services can make such schemes appear cost-effective in a way that cannot necessarily be replicated in mainstream delivery. There is also a need for comprehensiveness *over time*. The resource, reoffending and other ramifications of community and other penalties will not be exhausted within a single financial year, or even three or four years. Ideally, therefore, a cost or cost-effectiveness evaluation would span many years, taking in the full downstream implications.

Comprehensive costing raises conceptual and practical issues. In moving to a broad view it is not expected or necessary that each agency providing criminal justice services will use comprehensive costs in their decisions, but each needs some appreciation of them in order to understand the incentives at work within the system.

Tools

The PSSRU's research in the criminal justice area has relied on a number of instruments, often integrated into other questionnaires and schedules. Each instrument is a second cousin of the Client Service Receipt Inventory (CSRI: Beecham and Knapp, 1992), which has mainly been used in health and social care contexts. The CSRI provides a checklist of services that need to be considered, and what information needs to be collected about each of them (particularly frequency, duration, location and funding arrangements). The CSRI can also cover family costs, employment, household income and transfer payments.

Allen and Beecham (1993) describe a method for costing individual services - as identified by the CSRI or a management information system - that helps ensure comprehensive coverage. The first stage in their method is to obtain a detailed description of the service, identifying resources involved directly and indirectly in its production. The resources are defined as those required to produce the service in the long run whether or not payment is actually made for them in the short run. Costs may depend on context. For example, if a bail accommodation service is expanding, capital costs should be estimated on the basis of the need for new hostels; on the other hand, if the service is contracting, capital costs should reflect the market values of buildings that could be sold or their values in some alternative use. Units of intermediate output (volume or throughput) are then measured. Overall the aim is to calculate the long-run marginal opportunity cost of each unit of service (Knapp, 1993).

Using this approach, two main service types emerge - facility-based and peripatetic - with their own costing requirements. The approach has been used to collate *national-level* unit costs for community care services (Netten, 1994). An annual volume reports unit costs and the assumptions behind their calculation at a high level of detail to allow readers to make adaptations and to identify gaps in knowledge. This approach has also been used to provide a basic worksheet to identify information required to estimate costs for specific services (Netten, 1995; Dickey et al., 1995).

Many of the services in the criminal justice system, such as prosecution, are better described as processes. The costing procedure is similar: first get a detailed description of the service, then seek activity or output measures, and thus estimate the long-run marginal opportunity costs. It is important in this instance, however, to distinguish each stage in the process and to estimate the probability of a given individual moving through each stage. An example is given below.

Examples

Two experimental bail information and accommodation (BIA) schemes were established in Scotland to provide independently-verified information on the personal circumstances of bail applicants to assist bail decisions and to find accommodation for those who required it (Warner and McIvor, 1994; McIvor and Warner, 1996). The cost evaluation started with a detailed description of the processes and the paths through the system (Figure 9.2). The objective was to compare costs for those who went through BIA schemes with those who did not. It was hypothesised that the schemes might result in savings to the criminal justice system in two ways: by obviating the need for overnight remands for further enquiries, and through the prevention of unnecessary remands in custody pending trial (Netten and Knapp, 1994).

The next step was to identify the resources involved at each key stage. As the BIA officers were involved in a number of stages, not all of them relevant to every accused person, they were asked to complete time diaries for one week.

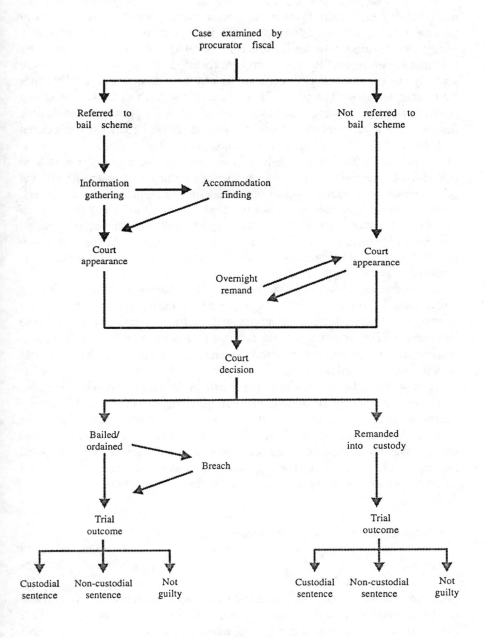

Figure 9.2: Routes through the prosecution and bail systems

These diaries identified tasks, persons contacted and, for professional or other public employees, the time taken in the contact and the tasks they asked others to undertake. This allowed estimation of the indirect costs to other agencies, in addition to the direct costs for the officers themselves, associated with compiling bail information reports for the courts. Accommodation placement costs were similarly based in part on time commitments by BIA officers and indirect costs from other agencies. The costs of time spent on cases which did *not* result in a report or a placement were added to the cost of successful placements so that the full costs of the schemes were accounted for. Additional costs were associated with developing and securing accommodation placements.

An important part of the study was to compare the costs of remands in custody with remands on bail. Comprehensive costing was essential. To the cost of prison were added the costs of services such as visits from social workers. The costs of being remanded on bail included (where appropriate) the costs of bail accommodation placements, income support, health care and social services. The costs of breaching bail, excluding the social cost of any offence committed, included the costs of preparing a case, overnight remands in police cells, prosecution and sentence.

One interesting finding was that the costs of maintaining an individual in a bail hostel exceeded the cost of remands in custody, primarily because of the much shorter period between the pleading diet and the trial for those remanded in the latter group. This, together with the fact that time spent on remand is taken into consideration when receiving a custodial sentence, meant that introduction of this BIA service generated no savings.

Each of the studies used as an example later in this chapter set out to measure costs comprehensively or, if this was not possible, to point out the missing elements and their likely effects on the conclusions. The latter was the case, for instance, in a cost study of community service orders (*not* reported here) in which it was not feasible to collect data on every trainee for every service used (Knapp et al., 1992), but where it was still possible to reach some useful conclusions about the component costs of this community penalty.

Establishing and exploring cost variations

Principles

Inter-user and inter-facility variations in cost are generally marked. They should not be ignored. To a degree, sentences and service packages purposively reflect individual needs, or at least individual offending profiles and histories, and a host of factors are likely to influence the associations between these characteristics and service use. Costs could be shaped by, *inter alia*, the preferences and perspectives of professionals and agencies, the bureaucratic tendencies of organisations, their scales of operation, and the characteristics of local areas. In consequence, costs will not necessarily be identical for two individuals given the same sentence, and one must have reservations about conclusions or recommendations based solely on *averages*.

The second evaluative principle is to explore and exploit these variations for their policy and practice insights.

Tools

There are three options when faced with cost (or effectiveness) variations: to ignore them, to over-ride them in an informed way (for example, through randomisation in choosing a research design) or to explore them with multivariate statistical methods. The third of these is the most satisfactory (although not inconsistent with randomisation). There exists a body of applied economics research which explores the reasons for cost variations, though rarely in criminal justice contexts. The good methodological route is to estimate a statistical cost function (Knapp, 1995b). The cost function builds directly on the economic theory of production, and hence flows directly from the production of welfare framework outlined earlier, and it is based on assumptions which have been examined in a variety of market and non-market contexts. In application the cost function technique has proved manageable and informative. It is commonly estimated for a cross-section of facilities or individuals using multiple regression analysis, with the dependent variable being total or average cost per user of unit of output, and with explanatory or independent variables suggested by theory and experience. The determinants of cost are selected in an empirical study on these same criteria plus statistical significance.

Examples

There is insufficient space here to give a full example of the cost function approach, but we can outline application of the approach at the facility-level, in earlier PSSRU work on prisons, and at the individual-level, for young offenders given (community-based) intermediate treatment sentences (Knapp and Fenyo, 1988, 1995). In both cases there were significant cost variations across a cross-section of cases (prisons or individual young people), and in each case a statistical cost function was able to 'explain' a sizeable proportion of the variation by reference to a number of factors suggested by hypotheses built up from economic theory and the criminal justice literature.

The examination of inter-prison costs relied entirely on routinely-collected and (largely) published Home Office data. Every prison establishment was included in the analyses, with the cost measure of interest being total expenditure divided by the average number of inmate weeks. A number of statistical analyses were conducted, with the eventual `final' cost function (selected on the usual mix of statistical, conceptual and pragmatic criteria) accounting for a high proportion of the variation in average costs. The factors found to have a statistically significant influence on average cost per inmate week were: average inmate population for each establishment; average occupancy proportion; staff shift scheme; establishment having one or more than one units; establishment having long term training facilities or not; proportion of places in special accommodation; proportion of places in dormitories; security categories of inmates; sentence length more than or less than five years; an index of mean sentence length (offence-weighted); number of previous offences per inmate; number of disciplinary offences within establishment; Central London location or not; transport facilities; and riot in previous year or not. Some of these factors were associated with custodial establishments and some with their inmates. The estimated prisons cost function had numerous uses, as arguments developed from any one of these significant associations would show.

The second example relates to young offenders. A recently-completed longitudinal study of more than 400 young offenders sentenced to custody, intermediate treatment (IT) or supervision order without IT (Bottoms et al., 1995) included a cost dimension. This illustrates how wide differences in sentence costs can be linked in part to offenders' individual characteristics, circumstances and offences at the point of sentence.

Separate cost prediction analyses were conducted for each of the three samples. We concentrate here on the IT group, whose sentence costs varied from £28 to £886 per week (and from £415 to £17,342 for the full period of an IT order; 1988/89 price levels). Statistical analyses produced estimated cost functions for weekly and period costs, distinguishing 'heavy end' IT (alternative to custody) and 'other' IT (HEIT and OIT). The analyses showed that 55 per cent of the weekly cost variation and 71 per cent of the period cost variation could be 'explained' by the characteristics of offenders at the point of sentencing by the courts. The estimated equations reveal many differences between HEIT and OIT, with few coefficients identical for the two groups.

Period and weekly costs are linked, respectively, to the length and intensity of an IT sentence, and both were found to be associated with the offences with which individuals were charged. (All crime-related measures for individual offenders were weighted by the availability to commit offences during the relevant pre-court period.) Threatening behaviour offences contributed significantly to the weekly and period costs of IT, whilst an offence of violence against the person pulled *down* the period cost for the OIT group, but not the weekly cost. The number of offences taken into consideration was associated with a slightly higher period cost, and both period and weekly costs were higher the greater the value of the property stolen and/or damaged.

Young people with mental health problems or learning disabilities, and those with solvent abuse problems used more services, as suggested by higher period costs of IT. There were links with educational status: other things being equal, weekly costs (but not period costs) were higher for those young people who - at the time of sentence - were not in full-time education, and costs were higher for those who had attended a residential special school. As with the effect of mental illness, the higher costs were not entirely to be found in relation to the community penalty (IT) itself but in adjunct services. A community penalty cannot directly influence the need for health care and education, but these needs might be dealt with and met differently (or perhaps not at all) in custodial settings, and perhaps dealt with differently by HEIT and OIT units. Clearly, therefore, the associated (comprehensive) costs need to be taken into account in policy discussions.

There were other influences on cost - other characteristics of offenders themselves, plus indicators of family structure, place of accommodation prior to sentence and area of the country - which together make it clear that the observed inter-individual cost variations are certainly not random. Cost differences can and, where possible, should be 'explained'.

Comparing like with like

Principles

Variations invite comparisons. Why is one IT user more costly than another? Why does one group of probation clients impose a greater burden on probation and other services than another group? Why is community service more expensive in some parts of the country than others? In addressing these questions, one must avoid drawing inferences from misplaced or misjudged comparisons, which was one of the reasons for conducting the cost function analyses described above. Like-with-like comparisons are needed to provide admissible evidence. Thus cost comparisons of offenders sentenced to prison with those on community service orders would need to be sure to focus on similar groups of people, for, in general, prisons contain more serious offenders than those given community penalties. Simply to compare averages could lead to erroneous conclusions.

Tools

The evaluative challenge, therefore, is to ensure comparability. In research this might be accomplished through randomisation, matching or statistical control techniques. It is not necessary to review the basic tenets of research design here, but it is as well to emphasise that like-with-like comparisons are as necessary in economic evaluations as in any other. To the best of our knowledge, there is no cost or cost-effectiveness evidence for UK criminal justice systems or services which is based on a randomised research design. In our own studies we have therefore sought to use multivariate statistical techniques - such as those described above - or, if the sample size does not permit this approach, careful matching of comparison groups. The latter approach can be illustrated with a study of reparation and mediation.

Examples

The reparation and mediation (R&M) study investigated the impact of two experimental schemes in Scotland intended to divert cases from prosecution (Warner, 1992). The challenge in the costing study was to find similar cases to those referred to the R&M schemes to estimate the resource implications of diversion (Netten and Knapp, 1992). The research design included the establishment of a comparison group to which half the cases suitable for one R&M scheme were randomly allocated, and information was collected about outcomes. It was not possible to cost exactly what happened in every case, but information was available about the characteristics of the group to inform the model of the prosecution process.

The prosecution process, like the bail information scheme was constructed as a series of stages or events, each of which was costed. This allowed estimation of the costs of different paths through the process, and calculation of an average cost by weighting stage costs with their probabilities of occurrence. Costs varied considerably depending on the path taken through the prosecution process. (The costing was limited to the District Courts as only cases to be prosecuted here were considered for R&M.) If the accused pled guilty at the pleading diet using no defence and no legal aid, the cost was approximately £37 (1989/90 prices). Incorporating assumptions about the probabilities of adjournment and legal aid being claimed, the highest cost was £1,119 (a case that came to trial resulting in an admonition). The cost was only £3 for those cases that were not prosecuted but sent a warning letter. Imprisonment was not included as a likely disposal unless it resulted from defaulting on a fine.

R&M was estimated to cost £298 per case in the scheme running at full capacity. For those cases that were not prosecuted (19 of the 44 cases in the control group) it was far more costly to receive R&M than to go through the normal criminal justice process. But for those who pled not guilty, which was likely to include those who are involved in complicated neighbourhood disputes, average costs of R&M were clearly lower (although the marginal costs of such cases are likely to be more costly to the R&M schemes). The average cost of prosecution based on evidence about the comparison group was £250, not much different to the costs of R&M.

Reparation and mediation schemes that divert accused from the prosecution process are sometimes presented as cost-saving measures. But the types of cases that can be dealt with in such schemes are often those that may not be prosecuted, or can be dealt with relatively quickly through the courts, or are likely to result in relatively low-cost disposals. This clearly illustrates the need to compare like with like if appropriate conclusions are to be drawn about the resource implications of alternative penalties or policies.

Costs and outcomes

Principles

It is inadvisable to separate discussions of costs and outcomes in the discussion or evaluation of community penalties. Ideally, the two types of information - the resource consequences, and effectiveness gauged in terms of re-offending and other dimensions - would be merged in every policy review, research endeavour or practice decision. The pragmatic second best is to recognise that one source of information is missing when drawing conclusions from the other. As we argued earlier, costs and outcomes are two parts of the same 'production of welfare' process – the inputs and outputs, means and ends, causes and effects.

Tools

Costs and outcomes can be examined together using one or more of a number of evaluative techniques developed by economists. The three most common are cost-effectiveness, cost-benefit and cost-utility analyses, and there are two variants: cost-offset and cost function analyses.

- *Cost-effectiveness analysis* (CEA) examines the costs of achieving a specified level of outcomes, for example a change in offending, and to conclude that the community penalty with lowest cost per given level of outcome is the most efficient or most cost-effective. This is not an easy rule to apply with multidimensional outcome measures, for if some outcomes improve and others deteriorate, or if the cost and outcome comparisons point to different 'best options' it is the task of the researcher to point to the various consequences and to leave decisions to others.

- A *cost-benefit analysis* (CBA) differs from a CEA in seeking to attach monetary values to outcomes. This may be sensible in some contexts, but

145

will rarely be feasible in criminal justice evaluations. While CEAs aim to show how a given level of outcome can be achieved at minimum cost (or maximum outcome at given cost), CBAs seek to discover whether benefits exceed or fall short of costs, and thus whether a penalty or policy option is economically worthwhile.

- A *cost-utility analysis* (CUA) is essentially a CEA conducted with a unidimensional outcome measure called utility. In health care studies, this latter measure is usually something called the quality-adjusted life year (QALY) - the number of healthy (or *partly*-healthy) years of life resulting from a course of treatment. It is not beyond the bounds of imagination to see a criminal justice counterpart, what we might call the *recidivism-adjusted life year* (RALY) - the number of years of post-sentence life adjusted for the frequency and seriousness of re-offending. A CUA would calculate the cost per RALY for different penalties, facilities, offenders or socio-economic groups. Any such measure as the RALY would harbour the disadvantage of loss of information consequent upon subsuming many different outcomes in a single scale. (In a different context - mental health care - Kavanagh and Stewart, 1995, discuss QALYs and also give a good introductory account of economic evaluative techniques.)

- *Cost-offset analyses* are comparisons of costs incurred with cost saved. Whilst useful, they do not conform to our fourth principle of integrating costs with outcomes.

- *Cost function analysis* was described previously, and can be seen as a multivariate generalisation of any of the other evaluative methods, although it is more searching in its exploration of inter-individual differences.

Examples

The study of young offenders introduced in section 4 collected both cost *and* outcomes evidence. The effectiveness of IT, custody and supervision orders was defined and measured by the Cambridge University team to cover: simple reconviction rates, amount of criminality in the year after completion of sentence (weighted for periods of unavailability because of custody), date of first reconviction or caution, and the impact on the juvenile as a person (Bottoms, 1995). They concluded that no one sentence or treatment type was better or worse than any other at preventing criminality. More favourable perceptions of IT than of other penalties were expressed by young offenders and their families, and there were some differences in reported social and behavioural problems in the year following completion of sentence for the custody group compared to the others.

The economic evaluation running alongside the Cambridge study included cost-effectiveness, cost-offset and (simple) cost-benefit analyses, and called on comprehensive cost evidence for both the sentence or 'intensive' period and the subsequent year (Knapp and Fenyo, 1995). The period costs are summarised in figure 9.3. The apparent cost differences between heavy-end IT and custody in the intensive and follow-on periods do not, in fact, attain statistical significance. (Statistical standardisation of between-sample differences, using cost functions of the kind presented above to make like-with-like comparisons, does not alter this conclusion.) In terms of comprehensive costs and re-offending, there is thus no evidence of IT being more cost-effective than custody, although the lower scores on the 'problems checklist' and the fact that costs are certainly not greater in the community setting may suggest a marginal cost-effectiveness advantage in favour of IT. Moreover, sentence length adjustments could alter this conclusion without necessarily altering the downstream costs or level of reoffending. This study also examined some monetary valuations of post-sentence offending (such as those reported by Williams and Anderson, 1975, and Home Office, 1992), again finding no marked differences between the sentence groups.

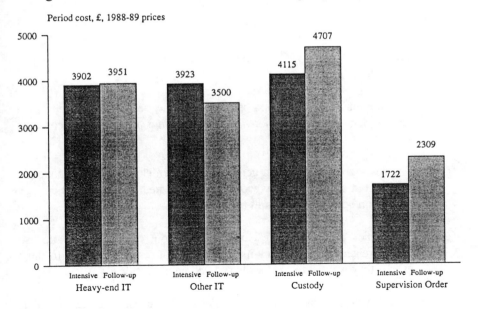

Period cost, £, 1988-89 prices

Figure 9.3: **Community and custodial penalties for young offenders**
   - period costs

Conclusion

We have set out the basic principles of cost or cost-effectiveness research in relation to community penalties, discussed some of the research tools that can be used, and given a few examples. Within a suitable framework, and built upon an accumulation of relevant experience, economic evaluations can be relatively straightforward to conduct, informative, and increasingly recognised to be essential. However, in the UK there have been few economic evaluations of community penalties or criminal justice issues more generally. Economic arguments have thus had limited influence on policy or practice. Why is this? A succinct summary of the problems of integrating economic arguments into criminal justice decision-making is suggested by adapting seven nested hypotheses which were first propounded, in a different context, by Alan Williams (published in Judge et al., 1983). We might postulate that:

(a)   Policy-makers do not believe (or recognise) the economic problems confronting or running through the criminal justice system as being researchable.

(b)   They do, but do not want to know.

(c)   They would like to know, but cannot wait.

(d)   They are willing to wait, but the research commissioning process is just not up to it.

(e)   The commissioning process is fine, but the research community in general has better (i.e. more enjoyable) things to do than economic studies.

(f)   The research community in general would be delighted to do economic studies, but cannot find any economists interested (or congenial) enough to take on board as colleagues to do such work.

(g)   Economic studies, even when carried out, are written up so incomprehensibly that policy-makers could not respond sensibly to them even if they wanted to, so they have become disillusioned.

We would suggest that hypotheses (a)-(c) should be rejected: there *is* recognition of the relevance of economic problems and studies, and policy-makers in the criminal justice area are probably as willing to wait for decent evidence as are policy-makers elsewhere. Hypothesis (d) probably cannot be

148

rejected. Very little research on the economics of criminal justice issues has been commissioned by central government or others, with the consequence that there is no 'critical mass' of accumulated research expertise. Our own studies, on which we have drawn for our examples in this chapter, have been sidelines - small-scale, opportunistic activities which we added to our mainstream research on health and social care. This is an unsatisfactory state of affairs. Unless and until there is adequate investment in economic expertise in the criminal justice area, there will be few answers to the many economic questions which changes of policy or practice necessarily pose.

References

Allen, C. and Beecham, J. (1993), 'Costing services: ideals and reality', in Netten and Beecham, op. cit.

Beecham, J. and Knapp, M.R.J. (1992), 'Costing psychiatric options', in G. Thornicroft, C. Brewin and J. Wing (eds.), *Measuring Mental Health Needs*, Oxford University Press, Oxford.

Bottoms, A.E. (1995), *Intensive Community Supervision for Young Offenders: Outcomes, Process and Cost*, Institute of Criminology, University of Cambridge.

Cm 965 (1990), *Crime, Justice and Protecting the Public*, HMSO, London.

Davies, B.P. and Knapp, M.R.J. (1981), *Old People's Homes and the Production of Welfare*, Routledge and Kegan Paul, London.

Dickey, B., Latimer, E., Beecham, J. and Powers, K. (1995), *Toolkit for Estimating Per Unit Mental Health Programme Costs*, Health Services Research Institute, Cambridge, Massachusetts.

Home Office (1992), *The Costs of Crime*, HMSO, London.

Judge, K., Knapp, M.R.J., Williams, A. and Wright, K. (1983), 'Resource implications of community care options', *Elderly People in the Community: Their Service Needs*, HMSO, London.

Knapp, M.R.J. (1984), *The Economics of Social Care*, Macmillan, London.

Knapp, M.R.J. (1993), 'Principles of applied cost research', in Netten and Beecham, op. cit.

Knapp, M.R.J., editor (1995a), *The Economic Evaluation of Mental Health Care*, Ashgate, Aldershot.

Knapp, M.R.J. (1995b), 'Costs and outcomes: variations and comparisons', in Knapp, op. cit.

Knapp, M.R.J. and Fenyo, A.J. (1988), 'Prison costs: why the variation?', *Home Office Research Bulletin*, 25, 9-13.

Knapp, M.R.J. and Fenyo, A.J. (1995), *Intermediate Treatment, Custody and Supervision Orders: A Cost-Effectiveness Study*, Personal Social Services Research Unit, University of Kent at Canterbury.

Knapp, M.R.J., Robertson, E. and McIvor, G. (1992) 'The comparative costs of community service and custody', *Howard Journal of Criminal Justice, 31*, 1, 8-30.

McIvor, G. and Warner, S. (1996), *Bail Services in Scotland*, Avebury, Aldershot.

Netten, A. (1994), *Unit Costs of Community Care 1994*, Personal Social Services Research Unit, University of Kent at Canterbury.

Netten, A. (1995), 'Costing breaks and opportunities', in K. Stalker (ed.), *Breaks and Opportunities: Developments in Short-Term Care*, Jessica Kingsley, London.

Netten, A. and Beecham J.K. (eds.) (1993), *Costing Community Care: Theory and Practice*, Ashgate, Aldershot.

Netten, A. and Knapp, M.R.J. (1992), 'Reparation, mediation and prosecution: comparative costs', in Warner, op. cit.

Netten, A. and Knapp, M.R.J. (1994), 'The costs of bail information and accommodation', in Warner and McIvor, op. cit.

Warner, S. (1992), *Making Amends: Justice for Victims and Offenders*, Avebury, Aldershot.

Warner, S. and McIvor, G. (1994), *Pre-Trial Bail Services in Scotland*, The Scottish Office Central Research Unit, Edinburgh.

Williams, A. and Anderson, R. (1975), *Efficiency in the Social Services*, Basil Blackwell and Martin Robertson, Oxford.

10 Evaluation methodology: back to basics

Ray Pawson

Introduction

This chapter serves a rather different function from all the rest. My purpose is to engage in a methodological crusade and to proclaim that it is high time that evaluation researchers went 'back to basics' in terms of methodological foundations. Arguments about programme effectiveness abound. This book will, without doubt, display a varying range of hopes and aspirations on what aspects of community penalties work. Without doubt, a completely contrasting collection could be assembled trumpeting the effectiveness of different types of custodial treatment. Without doubt, yet other voices still lurk waiting to declare that 'nothing works' in corrections, save for keeping offenders out of harms way for as long as possible. Disparity and disagreement is the norm.

There are, of course, a great many reasons for this typically confused state of affairs. Programmes can lead charmed (and not so charmed) lives - because of funding booms (and slumps), because of treatment fashion (or unconventionality), because of political friendships (and rivalries), because of career preservation strategies (or staff burnout), because of coherence (or confusion) between the aims and delivery of an initiative, to name but a few possibilities. No one can deny that such institutional realities sustain the roundabout of affirmation and denial on programme efficacy. Such thinking, however, leaves uncanvassed one of the more important factors in explaining the capriciousness of programme outcomes, namely that evaluation research itself has failed to deliver a clear enough knowledge base on what we know and can know about how programmes work. Evaluation research, from the 'Martinson' episode (1974) onwards, has produced highly ambiguous messages about the efficacy of corrections initiatives. Perhaps the time has come to blame the messenger.

Out with the old - the demise of experimental evaluation

The traditional message, of course, has been that evaluation should act as 'the experimental method for the experimenting society' (Campbell, 1969). Evaluation in the U.K. still trades instinctively on the time-honoured experimental design - the pre-test, post-test one control group design, which I reproduce as Figure 10.1 using Campbell's classic OXO notation. There is no need for me to explain the various steps in the procedure. I begin by extracting the underlying logic, which is that, being identical ($O_1 = O_2$) to begin with, the only difference between the experimental and control groups is application of the programme (X). Thus any difference in outcomes ($O_3 > O_4$) can only be that for which the treatment is responsible. To be sure, there are technical variations galore on this design but this is the basic logic of comparison through which evaluation traditionally gets done. So etched into the research mentality is its language of 'inputs', 'treatments', 'outputs' 'controls' and so on that it affects the very way we think of programmes. Rather than being made up of real people making real decisions, they become reduced to a unitary phase in such experimental sequences.

	pre-test	treatment applied	post-test
experimental group	O_1	X	O_3
control	O_2		O_4

Figure 10.1: The classic experimental design

Let me demonstrate this triumph of experimental logic over proper understanding by considering one of the classic objections to this basic design, which concerns the notion of random allocation. The random allocation of subjects to experimental and control groups is recommended in order to ensure that neither group has an abundance of characteristics which would predispose it to act favourably under the treatment. Now, in most of the programmes considered in this book, and in the 'corrections' area more generally, subjects enter programmes voluntarily. The people who are likely to be drawn into, lend support to, and (perhaps) be changed by the experience of a programme are those for whom it has salience. So, for instance, take a programme involving a considerable amount of co-operative group work or a long-term educational commitment, then assigning, by chance, one group of offenders to the programme and one elsewhere would lead to disruption of the initiative and maybe even its curtailment. One can summarise the point by saying that it is not programmes which work as such, but people co-operating and choosing to make them work. *Choice is the very condition of social and individual change and not some sort of practical hindrance to the understanding of that change.*

Now the experimentalist 'hears' all this but is still inclined to believe that since experimentation is *the* method, that the programme needs to be manipulated around the issue for a proper evaluation to be enacted. Thus the difficulties alluded to above are regarded as the 'volunteer problem' or as 'selection effects'. As a solution it is recommended that programmes should be evaluated by performing the experiment on volunteers only. Having made the choice that they want to be on a programme, offenders are then assigned randomly with some being granted their choice and others being allocated elsewhere. Dashing rapidly past the dubious ethics that this can sometimes involve, I want to inspect the results which typically follow from such an investigative strategy. Figure 10.2 contains some results from a Canadian pilot investigation of a 'cognitive skills' programme (Corrections Service of Canada, 1991).

I omit all details of the programme and the evaluation here and get straight to the methodological heart of the matter, which lies with the meaning of the three histograms comparing the readmission rates of (from the left) a) volunteers who made it onto the programme, b) volunteers who were dispersed elsewhere in the system and c) the base rate for the corrections system as a whole. What do the data reveal?

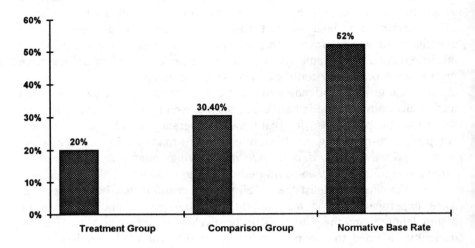

Figure 10.2 : The volunteer subject - some lessons from a Canadian study:comparison of readmission rates for experimental control and base rate groups

Let me offer three readings:

i)   The experimentalist's lesson. The experimental and control groups are identical right down to the fact that all have volunteered. The results thus show that the programme works and further evidence should be sought by replication of this procedure on a larger scale.

ii)   The bureaucrat's lesson. The biggest 'improvement' seems to be in the men who volunteered for the course but did not undertake it. A way forward for corrections would be to offer lots of courses attracting lots of volunteers but then not bother to run them.

iii) The real lesson. The course seems to have made a difference but for a self-selected group. The difference between the base rate and comparison group is just as instructive and future research will be equally valuable if it is aimed at understanding the characteristics of the volunteers and non-volunteers.

Let me say very rapidly (just in case a real bureaucrat reading this is on the look out for cuts) that lesson two is just me being facetious. Yet, in a way it is only half a joke, for readings one and two have close parallels in that they are both products of attending to evaluation by only having eyes for comparisons involving 'inputs' and 'outputs' of those undergoing 'treatment' and 'non-treatment'. Neither reading has any conception of the true implications of the diversity of subject's choices and motivations, which was the dilemma which prompted the illustration. The experimentalist instinct (as ever) is to regard such problems as 'noise' or as 'confounding variables' which have to be controlled by supplements to the basic design, before the real experimental apparatus gets rolled into place.

The real lesson is thus that 'volunteer only' experiments will enable one to pronounce on whether a programme works - without any knowledge of the make-up of volunteers. One is alerted to the crucial point that programmes tend to work more for some groups than others, but then the methodology directs attention away from an investigation of these characteristics. The issue at stake is thus a much more general one than the distinction between volunteers and non-volunteers. The act of volunteering marks merely a moment in a whole evolving pattern of choice which constitutes most social programmes. Potential subjects will consider a programme (or not), volunteer for it (or not), become interested (or not), co-operate closely (or not), stay the course (or not), learn lessons (or not), retain the lessons (or not). Programmes are thus learning processes and, as with any learning process, certain groups and individuals are much more likely to have the appropriate characteristics which will allow them to stay the course. Put more plainly, 'To assume that one treatment for everybody is going to work in the same fashion is crackers.' (Nuttall, 1992, p. 39).

This particular insanity is in fact part of a more general malaise. Experimental comparisons not only fail to ask 'for whom' a programme works but are also prone to neglect the issue of 'why' it works, a point made over a decade ago by Chen & Rossi (1983, p. 284).

> The domination of the experimental paradigm in the program evaluation literature has unfortunately drawn attention away from a more important task in gaining understanding of social programmes, namely, developing theoretical models of social interventions. A very seductive and attractive feature of controlled experiments is that it is not necessary to understand how a social programme works in order to estimate its net effects through randomised experiments.

Implied here is the suggestion that we should stop trying to think of programmes as singular 'treatments' which are present or absent. Rather, most initiatives (certainly of the type considered in this book) take the form of complex layers of social interaction which change over time. They are thus indubitably *not* 'dosages' in the middle of the OXO recipe, rather they contain a whole panoply of resources and ideas which might influence change in a subject's reasoning. Subjects will inevitably come under a myriad of such influences on a programme and any one of them may have the capacity to change them. The 'secret' of any initiative (and of all good practitioners) is thus to target the appropriate package of measures towards the appropriate subjects. Put more plainly, 'it is horses for courses' (Nuttall, 1992, p. 39).

This finally gets us to the nub of the methodological issue. 'Programming' is all about resources and ideas, subjects and choices. Within the experimental approach these tend to all get rolled haphazardly together in the one crude treatment versus control group comparison with the inevitable consequence that the programme *in the round* sometimes appears to 'work' and sometimes does not. One can in fact say that the better designed an evaluation in experimental terms (randomly assigned or particularly well matched groups with the experimental subjects undergoing identical or near identical treatment) the more likely are the net effects to be close to zero. Nuttall, in reviewing the influential 'San Francisco' and 'Impact' evaluations provides some classic examples of horses and courses getting hopelessly intertwined.

> ....positive effects with some people were cancelled out with negative effects with others...people who were less likely to reoffend (were) balanced out by people who were more likely to offend. Within the (experimental) group were people less likely to reoffend at the (programme's) end...but there were also people within the same group who were actually made worse because it was wrong for them. (Nuttall, 1992, p 39).

As a footnote I should mention that the case made here against experimental evaluation is necessarily brief, rather general and deliberately plain. The sceptical reader who might like to see the argument run in detail against a concrete and highly sophisticated experimental design should consult Pawson and Tilley (1994).

In with the new - the rise of scientific realist evaluation

Evaluation research mirrors social science more generally in the frequency of calls for a paradigm shift. The shortcomings of experimentalism of the type described above have led to calls for *Utilization - Focused Evaluation* (Patton, 1978), *Fourth Generation Evaluation* (Guba and Lincoln, 1989),

Theory Driven Evaluation (Chen, 1991) and so on. One influential new member of the evaluation repertoire, which I and a number of others have been urging on the research community, comes under the name of 'scientific realist evaluation'. Realism has a considerable pedigree as a philosophy of social science (Keat and Urry, 1975; Bhaskar, 1978; Harré, 1978) and has had a practical impact across a number of social science disciplines (Sayer, 1984; Pawson, 1989; Layder, 1993). Scientific realism's head start over other attempts to codify the rules of social research, is its commitment to ontological depth, that is to say, the notion that since social events are interwoven between various layers of social reality, then so must be any account of them. I have already noted this interplay of structure and agency which is involved in any social programme as the subject makes a choice between the different institutional pathways under offer.

Realism has suggestions to make on all aspects of evaluation research from design to policy making, data collection to analysis (see Pawson and Tilley, 1996 forthcoming). Its first task, however, is to provide a vocabulary for the understanding of social and individual change involved in social programmes. The basic elements of realist explanation can be broken down to the following (italicised) statement and a diagram (Figure 10.3).

The basic task of social inquiry is to explain interesting, puzzling, socially significant outcome patterns (O) between events or happenings or social properties. Explanation takes the form of positing some underlying mechanism (M) which generates these outcomes and thus consists of propositions about how the interplay between agency and structure has constituted these outcomes. Explanatory closure requires that, within the same investigation, there is also an examination of how the workings of such mechanisms contingent and conditional, and thus are only fired in particular historical or institutional contexts (C).

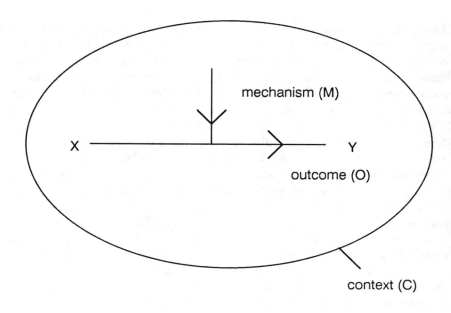

Figure 10.3: Basic elements of realist explanation

These 'ingredients' of explanation have a ready-made application to the field of evaluation. The notion of *outcomes* is, of course, already a familiar one in that it addresses the 'bottom line' question in all evaluation about the impact of programmes and so asks - did reoffending fall as the result of community penalties? - did crime fall as a result of the neighbourhood watch scheme? - and so on. The notion of *mechanisms* is close to the heart of all practitioners trying to make their initiatives work, but unaccountably absent in a great many evaluations. A mechanism is what a programme actually does to bring about change. Community probation schemes can operate to bring about change on a great many fronts, by increasing an offender's community awareness, by increasing employability, by increasing social skills, etc. Neighbourhood watch schemes can work by increasing surveillance, by strengthening informal social bonds, by producing publicity which drives the would-be offender off onto another patch, etc. To be sure such mechanisms do not offer universal panaceas - indeed they are only likely to be effective in rather special conditions. This brings us to the explanatory domain of the notion of *context*. Following the same examples through, we might say 'neighbourhood surveillance' might prove more effective amongst the twitching curtains of the terraced street rather than amidst the privet-clad privacy of suburbia, and we might say that 'probation as job training' is more realistic in an expanding labour market niche as opposed to a declining trade.

Bringing the parts together gives realist evaluation the task of hypothesising and testing explanatory propositions linking mechanisms to contexts to outcomes. All practitioners know that the difference between programme success and failure depends on complex and fine-grained conjunctions between these elements. To put it plainly, realist evaluation has the difficult task of spotting winners by finding the right horses for the right courses.

A realist research design

To the main point then, what will a realist inspired design look like in practice and how does this differ from a conventional OXO strategy. My case study concerns custodial treatment but since mine is a methodological tale, I trust the reader will forgive the inconsistency. I would wager, moreover, that it is not only the methodological lessons which are transferable. I take as my example some work in progress and thus lay open for inspection the design I have implemented, with others, to examine the impact of the Simon Fraser University Prison Education Program on the rehabilitation of inmates serving in British Columbian penitentiaries. The programme itself is unique, not least because it lasted over twenty years. The idea, to put it simply, is to install a *campus-in-a-prison* with several centres being established in which men could undertake a whole series of (preparatory, humanities and social sciences) university courses over a number of semesters and thus earn themselves credits over a number years towards a Simon Fraser degree. I describe here a vast programme which has involved over a thousand men and scores of teachers and co-ordinators.

The starting notion behind the design is that the Simon Fraser programme does not 'work' in reducing recidivism in some undifferentiated way. Perhaps the most compelling point to be made in respect of this is that for most participants on the programme (teachers and students), rehabilitation is not on the agenda as a direct and manifest goal. The guiding impulse has always been an educational one, namely to encourage as many men as possible, as far as possible, through a mainstream university education programme. Having said this, the research begins with the rather different assumption that non-therapeutic objectives can indeed have therapeutic outcomes. We thus start by assuming that the course can work and has worked in reducing reconviction. Putting it like this is no outrageous arrogance, but in fact a simple matter of anecdotal common-sense. Every co-ordinator on the programme is able to point to some individual - Joe Bloggs - who having been on the course, forsook a criminal career in preference for a lifestyle rooted in activities discovered whilst on the programme. I should add at once that such tales are frequently followed by accounts of other prisoners who have been academic 'stars' but from the moment of release have sought exactly the kind of trouble which has ensured an early return to the prison (programme).

In following the injunction to stop thinking of this or any other programme as some kind of unitary happening which either does or doesn't work, one has to admit to feelings of extreme trepidation. Attending this, or any other university course, comprises hundreds, thousands, millions of different events and experiences. We thus start with a situation which is surprisingly common in evaluation research - the possession of no singular theory about how our programme works to produce the desired outcome. This at least gives us a clear message about the principal task - namely to get on with it and generate such theories.

We can make a start on this in a rather abstract way by considering what we understand rehabilitation to 'be', before we get down to thinking about the details of those events which might be its spur. In higher education our weapons are the rather gentle ones of reasoning, thought and reflection. I suppose it is thus fairly obvious that notions of 'behaviour modification' of 'thought control', of 'deficiency repair' of 'curing the sick mind' are not really what we have in mind. Since coming on and staying on such a course is a voluntary action, we suppose that the rehabilitation process works through the medium of reasoning, of choice, of figuring-things-out-in-a-different way.

The process can thus be considered as a kind of pathway (see Figure 10.4) which begins with the offender in one spiral in which his social circumstances sustain and reinforce certain beliefs which act as a justification for criminal acts. Assuming that this spiral eventually spins the offender into prison, the rehabilitation programme faces the task of providing a new set of circumstances which encourage a new set of preferences and judgements and motivations. This new identity has to be powerful enough to be sustained on release so that the ex-offender seeks out situations which will foster the new non-criminal preferences. Putting it like this is no doubt an awkward formulation, but one I think which is instantly recognisable to many prisoners. One of our students on a British version of this programme (HMP Full Sutton) was able to put it much more simply. 'Barry Hunt then, is not the same as Barry Hunt now'.

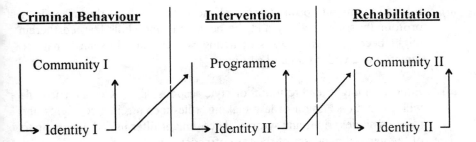

Figure 10.4: Rehabilitation as an intervention in the spiral of structure and agency

From the point of view of the research process, this model gives evaluation a much more authentic and better focussed task, namely to describe and explain the typical pathways or trajectories associated with rehabilitation. This sociological imagery of mutating spirals of structure and agency drives us much closer to the actual processes of social and individual change than does the input/output calculations across the OXO boxes. Realism, as I have argued previously, provides the counterpart methodological strategy to investigate these transformations. Firstly, it requires us to understand the mechanisms which prompt new ways of thinking which can in turn promote the gaining of a new identity. Secondly, it attempts to explicate those contexts which are more conducive (or more resistant) to change under the action of the mechanisms fired by the programme.

What is it about education which can provoke a prisoner into reckoning that a way of life they once considered justified, is justified no longer? The corrections literature is not short of answers to this question, nor on a more general plain is the philosophy associated with adult education. In a highly simplified way one can summarise some of the potential reintegrative mechanisms identified in these perspectives as follows.

i)   Education might be a spur to self-realisation. Following a particular course might lead to inmates developing knowledge, skills and confidence which realise their potential (for the first time).

ii)   Education might lead to economic potential. Education, of whatever sort can be considered to have a 'training' element which could act as a launch pad for providing a different set of opportunities towards a new career.

iii)   Education might promote social acceptability.   Education is a profoundly social activity and the behaviour and skills learned therein might become routine ways of acting which will allow an inmate to function in a wider range of settings.

iv)   Education might lead to moral or civic responsibility.   Certain curricula will involve discussion of law-making, rule-keeping, justice, rights and responsibilities, right and wrong.   These might filter in and become part of the general mind-set of the (ex) offender.

v)   Education might lead to cognitive change.   Education is perhaps above all about developing the reasoning process.   In confronting a whole new range of ideas, perspectives, and philosophies, the inmate's own power of reasoning and self-reflection might be deepened, encouraging a new outlook on old problems.

These goals are paraphrased here not because they are exhaustive and efficacious or even particularly wise and worthy.   Indeed, as everyone knows, they can be woefully far fetched in many prison contexts where there are a whole range of contravening forces in operation.   They are simply listed here as one of the prime tasks of the research project - namely to unravel the (combination) of personal, economic, social, moral or cognitive mechanisms which act as the engine for change.   Historically speaking, it is true to say that theoretical writings on the programme have tended to forward a 'cognitive growth' or 'moral reasoning' approach as the ultimate mechanism of reform.   These have their roots in (Kohlberg's) theories of moral development and Duguid (1981) in particular has argued that a liberal arts curriculum based in Literature and History is the most appropriate vehicle for this type of change.

In the present investigation hypothesis-making was not foreclosed around this particular dimension.   As I shall explain in a moment the real research design task is to transform this general agenda into a matrix for data collection.   Before I get down to these particular brass tacks, it is necessary to introduce the other major axis that impinges on our research design, namely the matter of how *context* conditions the potential for rehabilitation. In Palmer's (1975) terms we are now discussing 'for which types of offender, in what conditions and in what type of setting do programmes work'.   Although this is a missing element in many investigations, a moment's thought about the classroom will jolt us into realising its importance. The best educational course in the world (of any type) needs to have reasonably appropriate students to make the best of it. Accordingly, it is a common experience of all prison teachers that their courses attracts a 'certain type of prisoner'. All teachers would add furthermore that one has to be in the right institutional context in order to sustain the kind of priorities mentioned above. A substantial part of the research therefore can be considered to be about trying to specify those matches between course mechanism and the prisoners circumstances which are particularly conducive to rehabilitation.

Once again, it is the case that we do not have to begin the search for the answers to those who, when and where questions from scratch. The academic and practitioner literature is full of ideas on 'targets' for rehabilitation.

i)   Andrews's (1990) risk principle, which for some amounts to the 'first law' of corrections programmes, states that programmes invariably show most benefit amongst prisoners designated to have the highest risk of reoffending. In a prison education context this might involve the idea that those who are up to their eyes in criminal culture are invariably disadvantaged in social and educational terms. Placing effort here might provide more change than in prisoners who have experienced, if shunned, some social and educational advantage.

ii) Prisoner typologies are the stuff of many ethnographies which remind us that prison culture is not singular. Cohen and Taylor's (1972) rogues gallery, provides a useful example, and makes the following (fairly self-explanatory) sub-divisions - confrontationalists, symbiotic types, prison thieves, private sinners, situational criminals. This catalogue would raise a gleam of recognition to most prison educators' eyes who might be able to use it to suggest distinctions about who would prosper on and after the course.

iii) Prison organization itself, of course, is a response to the different characters and circumstances of the inmates. Thus we have young offender institutions, open prisons, dispersal prisons, training prisons and so forth as well as different security classifications for inmates within each establishment. Such managerial thinking impinges on the success of a prison education course at two different levels. Each of the potential mechanisms for reform through education above is going to have more (or less) scope according to the profile of the 'typical' inmate. Thus by dint of the age, offence, custodial record etc. certain establishments will have an 'availability' of suitable types. Regime differences will also bite at the institutional level and since prisons are also about security, surveillance and control, the precise 'ethos' of the establishment will limit the chances of success of any rehabilitation mechanism incorporated within an educational programme.

Such a listing of hypothetical contexts and mechanisms will always provide the basic ingredients of any real understanding of whether (prison education) programmes work. The quasi-experimental approach has failed to make progress because such hypotheses are not even countenanced within the basic design. What I need to demonstrate now, therefore, is how to incorporate them within a 'realist' research design. How this happened within the Simon Fraser programme is, I believe, a typical and, perhaps (by good fortune), exemplary practice. The design is illustrated in Figure 10.5. The best source of knowledge of the inner workings of a programme are generally speaking practitioners who have 'seen it through' for several years. In this instance (being a 'university' programme) the investigators are all practitioners or former practitioners on the programme. In general, realist investigation will not rely on rather broad hypotheses culled from the background literature, as above, but will also incorporate the 'folk wisdom' of practitioners who have seen it happen before their very eyes. [The broader theoretical parameters will be clarified over a number of investigations].

Qualitative	Quantitative	Qualitative/Quantitative
Inspection of practitioner's folk theories on why and for whom a programme works.	Outcome analysis internal to the programme of the particular contexts and mechanisms associated with success as predicted in 1.	Investigation of subject interpretation of programme to seek for a sense of self-recognition of processes described in 2.

Figure 10.5: Phases of realist evaluation

Immediately apparent in this particular design is the blend of the qualitative and the quantitative. Although this is a key feature of this particular inquiry, readers should not make the mistake of supposing that 'realism' is simply another way of expressing a desire for methodological pluralism. Realism is a *logic of investigation* and the following account stresses the contrast with experimental logic. Those key departures emerge with stage two of the design and so as to comply with space restrictions, I end this account there.

Readers interested in a realist account of the interview (stage 3) should consult Pawson (1995).

Phase one was implemented in the present case in a series of informal, *qualitative* interviews in which investigators asked practitioners (each other) to search their memory for cases, illustrations and patterns along the lines of *'what was it about the course which seemed to have the most impact in changing the men'* and *'what type of inmate is most likely to turn away from crime as a result of being in the programme'*. This released a flood of anecdotes and these tales from the classroom are remarkable not only for their insight but in terms of the explanatory form which is employed. These 'folk' theories turn out to be 'realist' theories and invariably identify those *contexts* and *mechanisms* which are conducive to the *outcome* of rehabilitation. Consider the following 'mediocrity' hypothesis which I paraphrase from the lips of one of the Simon Fraser co-ordinators.

> The men who are more likely to be changed are best described as mediocre. You shouldn't look for high-flyers. They are likely to be from a deprived background with a poor and maybe non-existent school record. They will be mediocre criminals too. They'll have gone on from petty crime, street crime to drugs or armed robbery or something. Then when they come onto the programme they're mediocre or worse. They just survive the first semester but then gradually build up getting C's and B's. So by the end, they've actually come a long, long way and that's what changes 'em. It is not so much a case of 'rehabilitation' as 'habilitation'.

It is worth inspecting closely what is being claimed here. It is a 'type' of offender and a 'type' of involvement with the programme which is said to be crucial. This example is presented here, of course, as a particularly rich and broad hypothesis deploying half a dozen or more distinctions to identifying the efficacious processes and backgrounds. This pooling of practitioners knowledge has given rise to dozens of equivalent, if somewhat more specific, hypotheses which we have tried to set down with some care in advance of the formal data collection. Space restrictions again require cutting a long story short and so simply naming some of these conjectures will, it is hoped give a fair indication of the contexts and mechanisms under investigation - the 'engagement' hypothesis, the 'improvers' hypothesis, 'the high flyer' hypothesis, the 'self-esteem' hypothesis, the 'protection' hypothesis, the 'breadth of learning' hypothesis, the 'second chance' hypothesis, the 'professional criminal' hypothesis, the 'drug dependency' hypothesis, the 'sexual deviance' hypothesis, the 'power' hypothesis and so on.

These qualitative preliminaries have the purpose of anchoring the later formal stages of evaluation. Thus phase one of the inquiry also has the task of creating a 'variable book' which seeks to operationalize these hunches and hypotheses in order to identify, with more precision, those combinations of types of offender and types of course involvement which mark the best chances of rehabilitation. Over fifty variables have been deployed giving me no chance here to describe the details of their construction and coding, but for the sake of illustration let me mention three examples. 'AGEPEP' (age of entry into the prison education programme) was the first candidate, following the evidence of our eyes that it was the 'calming down' set of the late twenties to early forties who had the motivation, patience and fortitude to survive the course. Variable 2 'EDUCENTRY' (grade, level, certification upon entry to prison) sustains a number of hypotheses including the idea that even modest university-level success for people with no post-secondary experience has a greater impact on self esteem than for those having had some taste of educational capital. Note also that via these hypotheses the men are differentiated closely (and somewhat more unusually) in terms of their different pathways through the course itself. Thus variable 23 'GPADIFF' (difference of grade point average across the first and second half of the course) enables us to pin-point the actual degree of 'improvement' or 'decline' of performance, and so chimes with 'greater-struggle-provides-greater-rewards' element of the 'mediocrity' hypothesis above.

Mention of 'operationalization' and 'variable books' will perhaps bring a sense of recognition to those inclined to favour more orthodox evaluation designs which do, of course, often employ statistical controls to supplement quasi-experimental comparison. I should take pains to stress therefore that the function of these variables is not statistical control as such. Crucial to this is the point that in identifying 'success', we expect it to be located in *complex configurations* of values on certain variables. So we will not rest content for instance in saying that 'age' makes a difference, or that 'type of offence' influences recidivism, or that 'improving Grade Point Average' is significant. The really marked levels of success will work at a level of complexity associated with the pathways or trajectories as depicted in figure four. They will be expressed by the likes of the 'mediocrity' hypotheses and will depict the coming together of a whole profile of subtle features from the offender's background as well a precise flow of experiences on the course.

This drives us several light years away from universal panaceas and, indeed, from the very notion that it is 'variables' themselves which do the explanation. For instance, in introducing the 'age' and 'prior education' variables, I did so via two bits of conventional wisdom about mature students, namely that they find success partly because they have reached a stage where, to put it metaphorically, hormones have given way to horse-sense, and partly because opportunities lost or never on offer tend to be more treasured than those handed to us on a plate. For one group of inmates, we suspect that age and education function in a completely different manner. This is our 'protection' hypotheses. A small number of younger convicts enter prison directly (or nearly so) from an educational background. These are usually first-time, serious, violent offenders A number of these are observed (hypothesised) to use the university programme as 'shelter' from the full rigours of prison life and this, if anything, intensifies their commitment to study. We recognize that this is one of the more remote pathways to rehabilitation, though our outcome data may just be able to detect it.

Note also, since there will always be winners and losers on any programme, that we suppose that some of these hypothetical pathways will mark relative 'failures' of the course, those parts of the criminal culture that education cannot reach.   Since, for purposes of targeting and future implementation such 'negative' findings are just as illuminating, it should be noted that we will investigate the programme's recidivists with (almost) as much gusto as the successes. For instance, one common tale about 'high-flyers' on the course (prisoners who establish themselves as good 'academics' and who also play a part in the 'politics' and administration of the programme) is that they often end up first in the queue of re-offenders. Perhaps they are already so well versed in the skills the course provides that they emerge unchanged, or perhaps they can only operate as big fishes in small ponds of which the outside world is not one.   Only careful identification of the group within the overall population will help us to remove these 'perhapses' and probably uniquely this investigation carries the inclination and records to find this out.

Phase two. The mixture of theorizing and qualitative investigation I have described so far is all preparatory to the main body of the investigation. The heart of the evaluation is an 'outcome' inquiry. Outcomes are all important in evaluation research because, of course, they provide the real answers to the ultimate 'does it work?' question. The first thing to establish in this respect is realism's quantitative credentials. Quite unashamedly, and quite orthodoxly, we can say that policy evaluation and implementation should turn on hard evidence and thus the primary task of any such research is to provide a valid quantitative picture of the successes and failures of an initiative.

Yet realist evaluation, as I have been at pains to point out, transforms the 'does it work?' question so that it is rendered 'what is it about the programme that works for whom?'. This gives the outcome analysis the task of building up a quantitative picture of which groups and which types of course experience are associated with lower recidivism. It asks, in short, which are the successful pathways? Outcome analysis, of course, is besotted (and sometimes bewildered) about measuring 'success' properly. Realism offers a rather subtle variation on the traditional theme here. In the present investigation, the spade work of the outcome analysis will be done by scouring the inmate's prison, programme and probation files. Lowering reconviction rates is thus the (traditional) measure of success to be used, with the expectation being that particular groups identified by the hypotheses and variable sets above will be associated with a clear pattern of reduced offending. The key device in operationalizing this measure of success will be the use of a *predictor scale*.

The scale in question is known as the SIR scale (Statistical Information on Recidivism). It was derived by Nuffield (1982) for Correctional Services Canada via the collection of data on the criminal histories, demographic characteristics and social background factors of prisoners, and relating these to reconviction rates. A statistical analysis was then performed to deduce those factors which best predict recidivism, and a well-established set of predictor variables has been identified which includes items like 'marital status', 'number of dependants', 'number of previous incarcerations', 'offence type', 'age at first conviction' and so on. These findings form the basis of the application into the SIR scale itself, which consists of a simple checklist of information to be obtained from inmates which allows them to be assigned into five risk categories. These range from the 'very good' risk group in which (only!) 1 in 5 offenders are reconvicted to the 'poor' risk group in which 2 in 3 reoffend.

Such information is now part of the normal case management documentation prepared for each prisoner and finds increasing usage in parole, release, and sentencing decisions. The surprising thing about such prediction scales is that they have found little use in one of the major roles for which they were originally designed - namely programme evaluation (Gottfredson and Tonry, 1987). The basic methodology could not be simpler (see Figure 10.6). Classification and prediction methods can provide estimates of the *expected* performance for any group of subjects and these expected outcomes can be compared with the *actual* performance of the group in the program under investigation. Thus the core methodology for evaluating prison education programme outcomes involves locating all inmates falling in explanatory categories such as those illustrated above and testing to see if actual reconviction rates are lower (or higher) than that predicted by SIR. Clearly such a method will allow for an 'overall' evaluation of the programme - as a whole did participants improve on the SIR prediction? The real interest, however, is in *internal variation*, we want to know if the particular groups, the 'mediocre', the 'improvers', the 'engaged', the 'second chancers' etc. turn out to be the real 'SIR-beaters'.

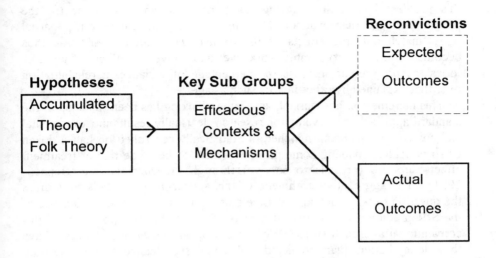

Figure 10.6: Outcome analysis - prediction scales

It is worth inspecting the logic embedded in the calculations here. In traditional (quasi-experimental) terms such prediction scales handle the problem of 'self-selection' or 'institutional selection' into programmes. That is to say, if a programme selects or attracts a particular kind of inmate who is already well predisposed to rehabilitation then quite erroneous claims can be made with respect to the efficacy of a programme. In general terms, university education programmes in prisons suffer from a bit of gross stereotyping in this respect. The image is of an elite groups of prisoners being cocooned from the harsh realities of prison life before being returned safely to their appropriate station. They can handle the courses in moral philosophy since they already have a good grasp of the Greek from their schooling. The beauty of a SIR based outcome investigation, in this respect, is that not only does it provide a profile of the risk categories of the Simon Fraser students (and will reveal, no doubt, that they are a rather typical bunch of 'villains') but also *that it takes these risk levels into account in numbering the successes.*

A brief, but important word, is appropriate here on what this phrase 'taking risk levels into account' means in this particular investigation. Let us take the example of the 'age factor'. Everyone knows that the ageing process itself can be considered as one of the greatest 'rehabilitative' forces

169

at work for the prison service. In Britain, for example, released inmates over the age of X return to prison at a rate of Y, whilst inmates under X return at a rate of Z Traditional quasi-experimental logic would attempt to confront this problem by treating 'ageing' as a rival explanatory factor to 'the programme' and then evaluate the latter by trying to 'cancel out', 'partial out', 'match out' the effects of the former. The outcome question thus becomes 'does the programme work over and above the effects of age', or 'does the programme increase the percentage of variance in rehabilitation over that explained by other factors such as age'.

This incremental, one-variable-at-a-time, thinking has been the bane of the standard approaches to evaluation research. It usually results in experimental and control groups being matched or statistically controlled on half a dozen or so variables, enabling some pronouncement to be made that a 'treatment effect' survives (or fails to survive) through the controls (e.g. Bennett, 1991). The aggregative arithmetic of this approach simply fails to address the question of why such an outcome pattern turns out as it did. Our use of the SIR predictor as a statistical control starts at the very point where this conventional approach stops. We can ask of *any group* we identify - have they done 'better' than predicted. The real significance of the question, however, and the power of the method lies in the subtlety of the identification of these groups. We will be able to examine the scores of combinations of 'prisoner type' and 'type of involvement' with the course which have been crafted in the preliminary qualitative investigation.

Because it is asked in conjunction with context and mechanism issues, *the realist outcome question is a different one*. Ageing is not considered as a separate rehabilitative process. Rather a particular group, a given age range (mid twenties to early forties) is identified as being conducive to certain particular effects of the course and is observed to see if that *potential is released* to levels over and above that which would have happened in the standard prison regime. Rehabilitative mechanisms are always contextually conditioned. It is the *conjunction* of particular aspects of the programme with particular characteristics of the prison population that 'works'. 'Ageing' is not a rehabilitative process as such. For that matter neither is 'education'. It is possible, however, that the process of bringing education's capacity for cognitive change to the context of the increasing maturity of inmates of a certain vintage, is rehabilitative. Then again, we have seen that 'age' might be influential as a different context under the action of a different mechanism. When education's primary role is to provide 'sanctuary' then educated, *young* first offenders can be expected to be the beneficiaries. Outcomes in evaluation research are always going to be internally complex and likely to be missed and mistaken in the additive, aggregative arithmetic of multiple regression. Outcomes in general thus need to be sought in this highly selective and pre-theorized fashion. And so whilst the evaluation calculation remains conventional enough (actual outcomes versus predicted ones) its content is transformed in realist inquiry.

It is always useful to clarify a new research strategy by attempting to capture its 'essence' and I should conclude with such an effort (lord help us, even methodology comes in 'soundbites' these days). OXO methodology has relied on the simple question about whether the 'treated' outperform the 'untreated' and discovered to its consternation that the answer is invariably - 'sometimes'. The realist strategy forces us to contemplate why and for whom a programme works. It is thus an approach which starts by differentiating the 'treatment' group and asks of the sub-groups so formed - DID THEY BEAT HISTORY OR REPEAT HISTORY? This, I submit, is not a bad place for all evaluation research to start.

Conclusion

The time has come to stress, once again, that the message of this chapter lies not so much with the example but with the methodology. Elsewhere, I have shown how a range of other designs in contrasting policy fields can carry the essential structure of scientific realist explanation (Pawson and Tilley, 1992, 1994, forthcoming). I conclude, however, by returning firmly between the covers of this book. One of the disadvantages of co-authoring a collection as one of twelve, is that one is left guessing as to what the other eleven will have said. It is appropriate, therefore, to draw to a close by turning this guesswork into a *forecast*....

Once again in the realm of programmes for offenders, research will have proved irritatingly inconclusive. Variations in programme effectiveness will have been discovered. Arguments for different outcome measures will have been made. There will be reports of implementation difficulties and unintended consequences. One suspects that the case for community penalties will remain 'yet to be proven'.

One reason for this is that programmes, practitioners and subjects (bless 'em) will forever remain stubborn, complex and difficult to follow. Another reason is that evaluation research has yet to organise itself around a consistent explanatory framework and research strategy. There is an urgent need for applied researchers to raise their sights beyond the demands of the current project and to examine the basic logic of evaluation. I trust this chapter has made a modest step in this direction.

References

Andrews, D. et al. (1990), 'Classification for effective rehabilitation', *Criminal Justice and Behaviour*, *17*, 19-52.

Bhaskar, R. (1978), *A Realist Theory of Science*, Harvester, Brighton..

Bennett, T. (1991), 'The Effectiveness of a Police-Initiated Fear Reducing Strategy' *British Journal of Criminology*, *13*, pp 1-14.

Campbell, D. T. (1969), 'Reforms as experiments,' *American Psychologists*, 24, 409-429.

Chen, H. (1990), *Theory-Driven Evaluation*, Sage, Newbury Park.

Chen, H. and Rossi, P. (1983), 'The theory-driven approach to validity' *Evaluation and Program Planning*, *10*, 95-103.

Cohen, S. and Taylor, L. (1972), *Psychological Survival*, Penguin, London.

Correction Service of Canada, (1991), 'Effectiveness of the Cognitive Skills Training Program: From Pilot to National Implementation', *Research Brief*, B-07.

Duguid, S. (1981), 'Prison Education and Criminal Choice: The Context of Decision Making', *Canadian Journal of Criminology*, *23*, (4).

Gottfredson, D and Tonry, M. (1991), *Production and Classification*, Chicago University Press, Chicago.

Guba, E and Lincoln, Y (1989), *Fourth Generation Evaluation*, Sage, Newbury Park..

Harré, R. (1978), *Social Being*, Oxford, Blackwell.

Keat, R and Urry, J, (1975), *Social Theory as Science*, Routledge & Kegan Paul, London. (second edition, 1981).

Layder, D. (1993), *New Strategies in Social Research*, Polity Press, Oxford.

Martinson, R. (1974), 'What Works? - Questions and Answers About Prison Reform', *Public Interest*, *35*, 22-45.

Nuffield, J (1982), *Parole Decision-Making in Canada*, Solicitor General of Canada, Ottawa.

Nuttall, C. (1992), 'What Works?' *Proceedings of the Annual Conference of the Association of Chief Officers of Probation*, Wakefield.

Palmer, T. (1975), 'Martinson Revisited', *Journal of Research in Crime and Delinquency*, *23*, 133-152.

Patton, M Q (1978), *Utilization - Focused Evaluation*, Sage, Beverley Hills CA..

Pawson, R. (1989), *A Measure for Measures*, Routledge, London.

Pawson, R. (1995 forthcoming), 'Theorising the Interview', *British Journal of Sociology*.

Pawson, R and Tilley, N (1992), 'Re-evaluation: Rethinking Research on Corrections and Crime', *Yearbook of Correctional Education*, 19-48, Simon Fraser University Press, Burnaby.

Pawson, R. and Tilley, N. (1994), 'What Works in Evaluation Research', *British Journal of Criminology*, *34*, 291-306.

Pawson, R. and Tilley, N. (1996 forthcoming), *Realistic Evaluation*, Sage.

Sayer, A. (1984), *Method in Social Science*, Hutchinson, London.